For better, for worse?

A report by the National Confidential
Enquiry into Patient Outcome
and Death (2008)

Compiled by:

D Mort MRCGP FRCR
Clinical Co-ordinator

M Lansdown MCh FRCS
Clinical Co-ordinator

N Smith PhD
Clinical Researcher

K Protopapa BSc (Hons)
Researcher

M Mason PhD
Chief Executive

Contents

Acknowledgements

This report, published by NCEPOD, could not have been achieved without the support of a wide range of individuals and organisations. Our particular thanks go to:

The expert group who advised NCEPOD:

Dr Peter Clark
Consultant Medical Oncologist

Dr Mark Ethell
Consultant Haematologist

Mr Matthew Johnson
Matron (Cancer Services), Lead Chemotherapy Nurse

Dr Fergus Macbeth
Consultant Clinical Oncologist

Mr John Marriott
Patient Representative

Dr Tim Perren
Consultant Medical Oncologist

Dr Tim Root
London Specialist Pharmacist: Clinical Governance
& Technical Services

Prof John Shepherd
Consultant Gynaecological Oncologist

Dr David Smith
Consultant Medical Oncologist

Dr John Snowden
Consultant Haematologist

Dr Stephen Whitaker
Consultant Clinical Oncologist

The advisors who reviewed the cases:

Mr Dermot Ball
Macmillan Network Pharmacist

Dr Frances Calman
Consultant Clinical Oncologist

Dr Michael Crawford
Consultant Medical Oncologist

Dr Jonathan Cullis
Consultant Haematologist

Dr Francis Daniel
Consultant Clinical Oncologist

Ms Susanna Daniels
Lead Pharmacist Cancer Services

Ms Jayne Davis
Lead Clinical Pharmacist Haematology

Dr Martin Eatock
Consultant Medical Oncologist

Dr David Eaton
Consultant Medical Oncologist

Dr Linda Evans
Consultant Medical Oncologist

Dr David Feuer
Consultant in Palliative Medicine

Dr Hugo Ford
Consultant Medical Oncologist

Mr Mark Gilmore
Oncology Nurse Manager

Ms Kerry Guile
Oncology Nurse

Mrs Meena Hunjan
Principal Pharmacist

Dr Graham Jackson
Consultant Haematologist

Ms Philippa Jones
Chemotherapy Nurse

Mrs Elaine Lennan
Consultant Nurse

Dr Pauline Leonard
Consultant Medical Oncologist

Dr Fiona Lofts
Consultant Medical Oncologist

Mrs Janet Miles
Chemotherapy Clinical Nurse Specialist:

Dr Jonathan Nicoll
Consultant Clinical Oncologist

Ms Catherine Oakley
Lead Cancer Nurse

Dr Marek Ostrowski
Consultant Clinical Oncologist

Dr Hamish Ross
Consultant Haematologist

Dr Paul Ross
Consultant Medical Oncologist

Ms Susan Sharp
Chemotherapy Specialist Nurse

Dr Bruce Sizer
Consultant Clinical Oncologist

Dr Steve Smith
Consultant Haematologist/Director of Cancer Services

Ms June So
Chief Pharmacist

Dr Nicholas Stuart
Consultant Medical Oncologist

Dr Jennifer Treleaven
Consultant Haematologist

Mrs Jacqueline Turner
Pharmacist

Dr Juan Valle
Consultant Medical Oncologist

The organisations that provided funding to cover the cost of this study:

National Patient Safety Agency
Department of Health, Social Services and Public Safety (Northern Ireland)
Aspen Healthcare
Benenden Hospital
BMI Healthcare
Care UK
Classic Hospitals
Covenant Healthcare
East Kent Medical Services
Fairfield Independent Hospital
HCA International
Health and Social Services, States of Guernsey

Hospital of St John and St Elizabeth
Isle of Man Health and Social Security Department
King Edward VII's Hospital Sister Agnes
London Clinic
Netcare Healthcare UK Ltd
New Victoria Hospital
Nuffield Health
Ramsay Health Care UK
Spire Health Care
St Anthony's Hospital
St Joseph's Hospital
States of Jersey, Health and Social Services
The Horder Centre
The Hospital Management Trust
The London Oncology Clinic
Ulster Independent Clinic

The professional organisations that support our work and who constitute our Steering Group:

Association of Anaesthetists of Great Britain and Ireland
Association of Surgeons of Great Britain and Ireland
College of Emergency Medicine
Coroners' Society of England and Wales
Faculty of Dental Surgery of the Royal College of Surgeons of England
Faculty of Public Health of the Royal College of Physicians of the UK
Institute of Healthcare Management
Royal College of Anaesthetists
Royal College of Child Health and Paediatrics
Royal College of General Practitioners
Royal College of Nursing
Royal College of Obstetricians and Gynaecologists
Royal College of Ophthalmologists
Royal College of Pathologists
Royal College of Physicians of London
Royal College of Radiologists
Royal College of Surgeons of England

The authors and Trustees of NCEPOD would particularly like to thank the NCEPOD staff for their work in collecting and analysing the data for this study:

Robert Alleway, Sabah Begg, Maurice Blackman, Heather Cooper, Sidhaarth Gobin, Kathryn Kelly, Dolores Jarman, Rakhee Lakhani, Waqaar Majid, Eva Nwosu, Hannah Shotton and Donna Weyman.

In addition, particular thanks go to Dr Martin Utley and Professor Steve Gallivan of the Clinical Operational Research Unit at University College London for their advice on method and analysis. Thanks also go to Clare Holtby for running the study.

DISCLAIMER

This work was undertaken by NCEPOD, which received funding for this report from the National Patient Safety Agency. The views expressed in this publication are those of the authors and not necessarily those of the Agency.

Foreword

Our contemporary culture does not deal well with death. There is great fear of cancer, and there is folk lore surrounding chemotherapy. Consequently, many fears go unspoken between the dying and their families because they are overwhelming. Conversations between cancer patients and their doctors are not easy either. Patients have an inherent desire to trust their doctor and to believe that something positive might happen; most doctors have a compelling desire to not distress their patients. These factors together can lead to some unfortunate management decisions, resulting in "doing something" - perhaps in doing anything - to not let such emotionally needy patients down. Revisiting these decisions in an enquiry is not easy either, but questions that are not asked are likely to go unanswered.

This report from NCEPOD (National Confidential Enquiry into Patient Outcome and Death) explores this territory. It asks difficult questions about what happened in the few weeks before death. At stressful times the option appraisal between doctors and patients can be difficult to unravel, and with hindsight all parties may wish something else had been done. There are some unpalatable findings about the decisions that emerged and the way in which they were made.

I must first spell out with absolute clarity that the design of the study is deliberately biased towards discovering things that might have been handled better. The starting point is a death that occurred within 30 days of having chemotherapy; this is a small minority of such treatments. Chemotherapy has transformed the outlook for many cancer patients who have longer and better lives. While the starting point is a death, that death may be completely in accordance with the very best medical practice. Death may have been due to the remorseless progression of the cancer but chemotherapy is toxic and some patients' deaths are hastened by treatment. We cannot put the clock back and treat only those who escaped that risk. Hindsight should be used with caution; there should not be over interpretation of any part of the report.

Oncologists have a more secure evidence base than many other areas of medical and surgical practice and constantly refer to trial data in clinical discussions. That said, why were only 4% of these patients in clinical trials? The philosopher Martyn Evans has cogently argued that trials are not an option but an obligation.[1] Oncologists have high quality evidence from clinical trials on previous patients; do not today's patients and doctors owe it to future patients to add to the evidence? We need trials of treatment in all contexts, including near end of life chemotherapy, on which to base future practice.

The study revealed a number of substantial concerns. We discovered unwillingness of some doctors to have their practice scrutinised – and an explicit avoidance of peer review. The return rate of questionnaires was lower than we are accustomed to for NCEPOD studies. Barely half the casenotes were sent to us and only two thirds of questionnaires, while we expect more than 80%. Repeated reminders were sent, from NCEPOD, Royal Colleges and the "cancer Czar", without much effect. The shortfall in returns might be put down to overwork (and oncologists are thinly spread) but some wrote that questionnaires would not be returned because only the treating doctor, not the multidisciplinary teams, and by implication, not NCEPOD could judge the appropriateness of treatment.

7

An issue was raised about who should look after patients in whom chemotherapy results in serious complications, and who should make that decision. Bound up with this is the recurring question about local care versus centralised care. This is to do with the conflicting pressures to return to a familiar team (ideally near home) or to be admitted to an acute hospital including an intensive care unit. The former seems kinder but some hospitals cannot provide treatment for septic shock which might require mechanical support of the lungs and kidneys. Even if you could plan from scratch and reconfigure all services, there is no one answer. If for example a patient aged 25 with a prospect of cure of 90% has a life threatening infection, ITU is the place to be. On the other hand if it was third line treatment of a lung cancer given more in hope than expectation, acute medical admission might be best avoided. The trajectory for most cancers is well known, so an explicit advanced plan for the level of intervention appropriate in the face of complications would be useful and any recommendation from NCEPOD should not override the role of the patient, family, and the general practitioner in sharing in the decision.

There remains a problem about how to put these choices to patients. For example, trials show about 5% more survivors at five years if chemotherapy is given after an operation to remove lung cancer. How do we put that to patients? Should they understand it to mean that of twenty patients so treated, one more of them will be "cured"? Or do we explain that on average patients live another few months? If it is the former the patient might consider the chemotherapy worth having. If it is the second, having their post operative recovery protracted by some months may not seem worth the gain. Some such patients are reported as deaths in this study and there is a concern that they might not have had sufficient information to allow them to balance the burdens and benefits of the treatment.

The topics chosen for study by NCEPOD arise from concerns expressed by health professionals and the public; they are studied in a detailed process of qualitative and quantitative analysis by panels representing medical and non-medical view points - and we pull no punches in our recommendations. If there is a feeling that things are not as good as they could be, or that there are recurring themes of worrying practice or outcomes, these are matters we study.[2] Chemotherapy near the end of life (in the event, not by intent) is a prime example. The public and patients with experience of a family member, whose death and chemotherapy were close in time, summarise this all too readily: "they gave her chemotherapy but she was dead in a couple of weeks". There are all sorts of undertones of inappropriateness, futility, money wasted, medical desire to be seen to be doing something, even heartlessness, and straw clutching. These merit careful consideration and suggestions as to how things could be better. We hope that this report will help inform this debate so that patients benefit.

Professor T Treasure, NCEPOD Chairman

(1) Evans HM. Should patients be allowed to veto their participation in clinical research? J Med Ethics 2004; 30(2):198-203.

(2) Treasure T. Are patients safe with the NHS? Science in Parliament: the Journal of the Parliamentary and Scientific Committee 2007; Spring 2007(Spring 2007):26-27.

Principal Recommendations

Hospital facilities

Hospitals that treat patients with SACT but do not have the facilities to manage patients who are acutely unwell should have a formal agreement with another hospital for the admission or transfer of such patients as appropriate. *(Medical directors)*

Decision to treat

There must be greater standardisation of the consent form. The name and grade of doctors taking consent should always be stated on the consent form. *(Cancer services managers, clinical directors and medical directors)*

Consent should only be taken by a clinician sufficiently experienced to judge that the patient's decision has been made after consideration of the potential risks and benefits of the treatment, and that treatment is in the patient's best interest. *(Clinical directors)*

Giving palliative SACT to poor performance status patients grade 3 or 4 should be done so with caution and having been discussed at a MDT meeting. *(Consultants)*

SACT prescriptions and administration

Junior medical staff at FY1, FY2, ST1 and ST2 grade should not be authorised to initiate SACT. *(Clinical directors)*

Pharmacists should sign the SACT prescription to indicate that it has been verified and validated for the intended patient and that all the safety checks have been undertaken. *(Pharmacists)*

Safety of SACT

Consultants should follow good clinical practice and consider:-
- Reducing the dose of SACT in patients
  - that have received a number of previous courses of treatment
  - that have a poor performance status
  - that have significant co-morbidity;
- Reducing the dose of or omitting drugs excreted via the kidney, if the patient has impaired renal function;
- Reducing the dose of, or omitting, drugs excreted via the liver, if the patient has impaired liver function. *(Consultants and clinical directors)*

Hospital admissions during the last 30 days of life

Emergency admissions services must have the resources to manage SACT toxicity. These should include:-
- A clinical care pathway for suspected neutropenic sepsis;
- A local policy for the management of neutropenic sepsis;
- Appropriately trained staff familiar with the neutropenic sepsis policy;
- A policy that should be easily accessible in all emergency departments;
- Availability of appropriate antibiotics within the emergency department. *(Cancer services managers and clinical directors)*

In planning the provision of oncology services outside of cancer centres, commissioners should take into account the need for specialist advice to be readily available when patients are admitted acutely. *(Cancer services managers)*

End of life care

A pro-active rather than reactive approach should be adopted to ensure that palliative care treatments or referrals are initiated early and appropriately: Oncologists should enquire, at an appropriate time, about any advance decisions the patient might wish to make should they lose the capacity to make their own decisions in the future. *(Consultants)*

Regular clinical audit should be undertaken on the management of all cases of neutropenic sepsis following the administration of SACT. The process of care should be compared to standards agreed by the cancer network. Cancer centres and cancer units should collaborate in undertaking these audits. *(Clinical directors)*

All deaths within 30 days of SACT should be considered at a morbidity and mortality or a clinical governance meeting. *(Clinical directors and consultants)*

Personnel named in brackets after each recommendation are those NCEPOD believes are most appropriate to act on the recommendation.

Introduction

The National Confidential Enquiry into Patient Outcome and Death (NCEPOD) has performed a study on the use of systemic anti-cancer therapy (SACT) in both palliative and potentially curative clinical management plans. The aim of palliative treatment is to relieve or delay the onset of symptoms. Consequently drug doses are adjusted in order to minimise any treatment related toxicity. In potentially curative treatments, maximum tolerated drug doses are used in order to achieve greater efficacy. However, these treatment regimens can be associated with a greater risk of morbidity and possible mortality.

Potential side effects of treatment include nausea and vomiting, mouth ulceration, diarrhoea, hair loss and bone marrow depression. Treatment related toxicities range in severity and are graded using the Common Toxicity Criteria (Appendix 5). Adjustments to the dose and timing of treatment and the prophylactic use of anti-emetics, antibiotics and bone marrow stimulants have resulted in a reduction in the severity of side effects. However, one of the most serious complications of treatment is neutropenic sepsis. Bone marrow depression leads to a reduction in the number of neutrophils in the peripheral blood and the immune system's ability to combat infection. Systemic infection as a result of neutropenia can be life threatening. Patients may also suffer serious complications associated with the route of drug administration, for example, central venous line infections or thromboses and associated life threatening pulmonary emboli.

Throughout this report, the following national clinical guidelines on the management of cancer and the use of SACT have been used as standards where possible:

- The Department of Health's Manual for Cancer Services - chemotherapy section, against which the delivery of the chemotherapy service was assessed during peer review[1];
- The Clinical Oncology Information Network (COIN) project which promotes effective clinical practice in oncology and was sponsored by the Faculty of Clinical Oncology of The Royal College of Radiologists (RCR) and the Joint Collegiate Council for Oncology (JCCO)[2,3];
- Chemotherapy guidelines produced by the British Committee for Standards in Haematology (BCSH)[4];
- The National Institute for Health and Clinical Excellence (NICE) cancer service guidance, clinical guidelines and technology appraisals[5-7].

Although clinical outcomes following treatment of cancer and haematological malignancies are improving, there was concern that the quality of care was not of a consistently high standard across the UK. The Joint Specialty Committee (JSC) of Medical Oncology of the Royal College of Physicians, supported by the JCCO, submitted a cancer study proposal to NCEPOD in February 2005. The topic was selected by the Steering Group and the project commenced in January 2006.

NCEPOD studied the death of those patients who died within 30 days of treatment, looking at whether the death was due to treatment related toxicity, progression of malignant disease or an unrelated cause. NCEPOD looked for remediable factors in the process of care in the prescribing and administration of SACT in the clinical care following development of toxicity and the initial decision to treat with SACT. This study also assessed the resources available for the non surgical management of malignant disease, patient information, the use of local clinical care pathways and clinical governance programmes.

This study involved the collation of data on resources and clinical policies within individual hospitals. The presentation of some of the organisational data is related to service provision – clinical/medical oncology or haemato-oncology, as these services are often provided by different units.

All of the study group patients died within 30 days of treatment and therefore the group was not a representative sample of the total population receiving SACT.

The oncology service

The non surgical oncology service is provided by specialist oncologists.

Clinical oncologists are members of the Royal College of Radiologists (Oncology section) who have undergone specialist training in the provision of radiotherapy and chemotherapy.

Medical oncologists are members of the Royal College of Physicians and have specialist training in the management of malignancies using chemotherapy.

Both clinical and medical oncologists are based in cancer centres with peripheral clinics in cancer units. They work together as teams specialising in specific tumour types.

Haemato-oncologists are members of both the Royal College of Physicians and Royal College of Pathologists, who have undergone specialist training in haematology and the management of haematological malignancies. They are usually based within the haematology departments of large teaching and district general hospitals.

1 – Method

Expert group

An expert group was convened following nominations from relevant Royal Colleges and specialist Societies. The group comprised medical and clinical oncologists, haemato-oncologists, a gynaecological oncologist, a palliative medicine physician, a pharmacist, a specialist chemotherapy nurse, and a patient representative. The members contributed to the preparation of the study protocol and design of data collection forms. The group defined the aims and objectives of the study, reviewed the analyses of the data and commented on the initial drafts of the report.

Independent advice on the study method and data analysis was provided by the Clinical Operational Research Unit (CORU) at University College London (UCL).

Study aim

The aim of this study was to examine the process of care of patients who died within 30 days of receiving systemic anti-cancer therapy (SACT) in order to identify remediable factors in the care received by these patients.

Objectives

Six key areas of interest were identified that would address the overall aim of the study:
- The appropriateness of the decision to treat with SACT;
- The process of care in the prescribing and administration of SACT;
- The safety of care in the monitoring of toxicity and managing complications;
- End of life care;
- Communication - patient information, multidisciplinary team (MDT) working, referral pathways;
- Clinical governance, clinical audit and risk management issues.

Hospital participation

National Health Service hospitals in England, Wales and Northern Ireland were expected to participate, as well as hospitals in the independent sector and public hospitals in the Isle of Man, Guernsey and Jersey.

Within each hospital, a named contact, referred to as the NCEPOD Local Reporter, acted as a liaison between NCEPOD and the hospital staff, facilitating case identification, dissemination of questionnaires and data collation.

Pilot study

To test the feasibility of certain aspects of the study, a pilot study was conducted in September 2006. This assessed:
- The methods used and the ease of obtaining data;
- The appropriateness of the questionnaires;
- The incidence of deaths within 30 days of SACT.

Twenty six hospitals participated in the pilot study. Hospitals were selected to ensure a range of sizes and types of hospital. Each hospital was asked to complete an organisational questionnaire and comment on the content and format.

The NCEPOD Local Reporter at each hospital was asked to identify all patients treated with SACT between 1st September 2006 and 30th September 2006 and provide data regarding the date of SACT and date of death if applicable.

Within each hospital, two or three cases of patients who had died within 30 days of SACT were chosen by NCEPOD for detailed review. The cases were selected to ensure a range of different tumour types. The local consultants were requested to complete and comment on the clinical questionnaires and the NCEPOD staff used photocopied casenote extracts to undertake a detailed review of the patients' care and assess the ease of completion of the assessment form.

Main study

Study population
Data were collected on patients who were treated with SACT between 1st June 2006 and 31st July 2006 inclusive and on patients who died between 1st June 2006 and 31st August 2006 inclusive.

Inclusion criteria
1   Patients aged 16 years or over; who had
2   Solid tumours or haematological malignancies; who then
3   Received intravenous, oral, subcutaneous, intravesical, intrathecal, or intraperitoneal chemotherapy, monoclonal antibodies or immunotherapy during the study period; and
4   Who died within 30 days of receiving SACT, either in hospital or in the community.

The 30 day period was defined as 30 days from the first day of the SACT cycle immediately prior to death. When SACT was given continuously, then the 30 day period was defined as death within 30 days of the date of the last prescription.

Exclusion criteria
The following groups of patients were excluded from the study:
*   Patients in Phase I trials;
*   Patients receiving hormone therapy alone;
*   Patients receiving vaccines;
*   Patients receiving gene therapy.

Case ascertainment
The following data collection methods were used.

The NCEPOD Local Reporter liaised with the hospital pharmacist to identify patients who received SACT between 1st June 2006 and 31st July 2006 inclusive. The data were entered onto a spreadsheet provided by NCEPOD.

The NCEPOD Local Reporter identified all patients who died within their hospital, regardless of disease type or disorder, between 1st June 2006 and 31st August 2006 inclusive and entered the data onto the same spreadsheet.

An exercise was undertaken by NCEPOD to identify all patients who had died within 30 days of SACT administration. A list of patients who had received SACT but had not died in hospital was supplied to the Office for National Statistics who identified patients who had died out of hospital.

Questionnaires and casenotes

Organisational questionnaire

An organisational questionnaire was sent to every hospital that had informed NCEPOD that SACT was administered on site. Information was collected at hospital level as it gave a better indication of the facilities available for a patient at the location where they were receiving care, rather than all the facilities available within a multi-hospital trust. This questionnaire allowed data to be collected concerning staff numbers, departmental facilities and local clinical care protocols for each participating hospital.

Questionnaire A - Treatment plan and administration

This questionnaire was sent to the consultant responsible for initiating the most recent course of SACT.

Questionnaire B - Follow-up, toxicity and death

For patients who died in hospital, this questionnaire was sent to the consultant responsible for the care of the patient at the time of death.

For patients who died in the community, the questionnaire was sent to the consultant responsible for initiating the most recent course of SACT.

Casenotes

Photocopies of extracts of the medical record were requested. These included:
- Data related to the most recent course of SACT
- The complete casenotes for the last 30 days of life:
  - Inpatient and outpatient annotations - medical and nursing
  - Drug charts
  - Observation charts
  - Notes from MDT meetings
  - Correspondence between health care professionals
  - Operation notes

- Pathology results
- Radiology investigation results
- Consent forms for SACT
- Chemotherapy prescriptions
- Radiotherapy prescriptions
- Haematology biochemistry results) for last course of SACT (this may have included a number of cycles)
- Creatinine clearance
- Tumour marker results (CEA, CA 19-9, CA 125, CA 153, PSA, AFP, BHCG)
- Do not attempt resuscitation (DNAR) orders
- End of Life Care Pathway documentation
- Incident report form and details of outcome
- Autopsy report

Assessment form

Key data from the casenotes were extracted by non-clinical staff at NCEPOD and recorded on the assessment form (AF) in order to construct a patient journey. The rest of the form was completed by clinical advisors during their detailed review of each case. Expert opinion on the care provided was recorded.

Advisor groups

A multidisciplinary group of advisors was selected to review the completed questionnaires and casenotes. The group of advisors comprised haemato-oncologists, medical and clinical oncologists, a palliative medicine physician, pharmacists and specialist chemotherapy nurses.

All questionnaires and casenotes were anonymised by the non-clinical staff at NCEPOD. All identifying information relating to the patient, medical staff and hospital were removed. No clinical staff at NCEPOD, nor advisors, had access to any information that would allow patients, clinical staff of hospitals to be identified.

Following anonymisation, each case was reviewed by an oncologist or haemato-oncologist as appropriate, followed by a pharmacist and a nurse. The cases were often very complex and review by three advisors allowed the process to be as thorough as possible. Cases where it was difficult to reach a decision regarding care received were discussed within the group of advisors and a consensus reached.

The following system was used by the advisors to grade the overall care provided:

1   **Good practice:** A standard that you would accept from yourself, your trainees and your institution.

2   **Room for improvement:** Aspects of *clinical care* that could have been better.

3   **Room for improvement:** Aspects of *organisational care* that could have been better.

4   **Room for improvement:** Aspects of both *clinical care* and *organisational care* that could have been better.

5   **Less than satisfactory:** Several aspects of *clinical* and/or *organisational care* that were well below a standard that you would accept from yourself, your trainees and your institution.

6   **Insufficient information:** Insufficient information available to assess the quality of care.

At regular intervals throughout the advisors meetings, the NCEPOD clinical co-ordinator facilitated discussion. All grade 5 cases were discussed in detail as well as recurrent areas of concern identified in grade 2, 3 and 4 cases.

Quality and confidentiality

Missing casenotes that were essential to the peer review process were requested again if not initially returned to NCEPOD. When the data were as complete as possible, the identifying casenote number (and any other identifiable information) on each questionnaire was removed. Each case was assigned a unique NCEPOD number so that cases could not be easily linked to a hospital.

The data from all the questionnaires and assessment forms were electronically scanned into a preset database. Prior to any analysis taking place, the dataset was cleaned to ensure that there were no duplicate records and that erroneous data had not been entered during scanning. All data were then validated by NCEPOD non-clinical staff.

Data analysis

Quantitative data were analysed using Microsoft Access and Excel by the NCEPOD staff.

The qualitative data collected from the questionnaires were coded according to context. These data were reviewed by NCEPOD clinical staff to identify recurring themes. Some of these have been highlighted within the report using case studies.

The findings of the study were reviewed by the expert group, advisors and the NCEPOD Steering Group prior to publication.

2 – Data overview

Hospital participation

Information on hospital deaths and administration of SACT was requested from 1051 hospitals.

SACT data

NCEPOD was notified by 667/1051 (64%) hospitals as to whether or not they treated patients with SACT: in 366 hospitals patients were treated, from which 304/366 (83%) hospitals returned a spreadsheet containing patient identifiers and dates of administration of SACT.

Death data

NCEPOD were notified by 901/1051 (86%) hospitals whether deaths had occurred during the study period. Of these, 600 returned a spreadsheet containing data on patient identifiers and dates of death.

Organisational questionnaire

An organisational questionnaire was sent to all hospitals (366) that indicated that they administered SACT on site. A completed questionnaire was returned from 295/366 (81%) hospitals.

Sample selection

47,050 SACT treatments were reported to NCEPOD during the study time period (June and July 2006) and 55,710 deaths from any cause (June to August 2006). From these data 1415 deaths within 30 days of treatment were identified: 1063 from hospital data and 352 from further matching using data from the Office for National Statistics. Of these cases, 371 were subsequently excluded. The reasons for exclusion can be found in Table 2.1.

Table 2.1 Reasons for exclusion

Reason for exclusion	Number of cases
Patient still alive	2
Patient aged under 16	4
Non cancer patient	15
Day of SACT administration outside study period	43
Patient did not receive SACT e.g. delayed due to illness	121
Patient died outside of the study period	186
Total	371

Clinical questionnaire returns

Figure 2.1 highlights the compliance rate in the return of questionnaires A, B and the casenotes.

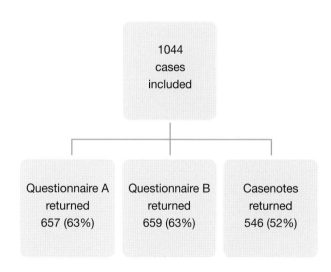

Figure 2.1 Data returns

Only 478/1044 (46%) cases had both questionnaires and casenotes returned. A further 189 had questionnaires returned but no casenotes and therefore could not be assessed by the advisors but were included in the analysis where appropriate. In total 546 cases were reviewed by the advisors as there were sufficient casenotes and, but not necessarily, at least one clinical questionnaire.

In 118 cases, the patient died at a different hospital to the one where they received SACT and therefore had two sets of casenotes. If both sets were not returned, only part of the clinical history was available for review.

Data analysis

Denominators for this report will either be 546 when considering the advisors' opinion of the casenotes plus one or more clinical questionnaires; or 657 or 659 when considering the data returned to NCEPOD from questionnaire A or B respectively. However, the denominators may also change if some questions had not been answered fully or where different analyses were dependent on different sources of data, and this will be noted throughout the report. The denominator for organisational questionnaires will be 295.

In addition to the data analyses a number of case studies have also been used to illustrate the clinical relevance of the data presented. These case studies were taken from themes arising from the advisors' meetings and each case study is an amalgamation of more than one case that had a similar clinical theme.

The overall return rate for all questionnaires and casenotes for this study was lower than that for previous NCEPOD studies which usually exceeds 70-80%[8,9]. Reminder letters were sent to individual clinicians and to trust medical directors. In addition a letter signed by the Chairman of NCEPOD, the National Cancer Director and the Royal College of Radiologists was sent to all clinicians who had not returned questionnaires to outline the importance of this study. These reminders had very little effect. This may have been due to lack of time made available during the working week to complete the questionnaires or perhaps a lack of willingness to contribute to peer review. Contribution to confidential enquiries to help reduce risk to patients is considered an overriding duty by the General Medical Council[10].

Although participation was lower than expected, the number of cases reviewed and the methodology used by NCEPOD still identifies ways in which delivery of SACT can fall below the standard we strive for and what we might do to remedy this.

Overall standard of care

The NCEPOD grading system for overall standard of care is outlined in Chapter 1. Care was graded by the advisors and ranged from good practice to less than satisfactory, with various grades of room for improvement in between.

The advisor ratings of the care provided can be seen in Figure 2.2:

35% of patients received care judged by the advisors as good.

38% of patients had room for improvement in clinical care.

6% of patients had room for improvement in organisational care.

5% of patients had room for improvement in both clinical and organisational care.

8% of patients received less than satisfactory care.

8% of patients had insufficient data available to assess the case.

Number of Patients

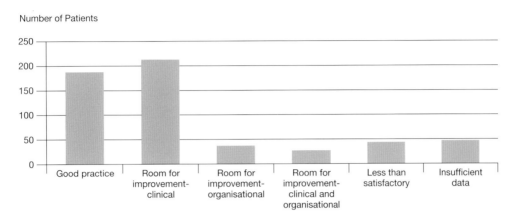

Figure 2.2 Overall assessment of care - advisors' opinion

When compared to previous NCEPOD studies using the same grading system[7,8,11-15], this is the first time that room for clinical improvement has been greater than good practice. Although the patients in this study are not representative of patients receiving SACT as a whole, this finding must lead to continuing debate on how to improve the service to patients with cancer.

Key findings

The clinical questionnaire return rate was low (63%) despite reminder letters to individual consultants and medical directors. This is below the standard expected for NCEPOD studies.

In 35% of patients who died within 30 days of receiving SACT, care provided was judged as good.

In the advisors' opinion there was room for improvement in the care provided to 49% of patients who died within 30 days of receiving SACT.

In 8% of cases the care provided was less than satisfactory. In the advisors' opinion the care was well below an acceptable standard.

Recommendation

Cancer services managers and clinical directors must ensure that time is made available in consultants' job plans for clinical audit. They must also ensure that the time allocated is used for the defined purpose. *(Cancer services managers and clinical directors)*

3 – Hospital resources

Introduction

In this chapter the resources at the disposal of hospitals that administer systemic anti-cancer therapy (SACT) are described. It is based on information from the 295 completed organisational questionnaires.

The infrastructure required for the delivery of SACT to patients with haematological malignancies is in many ways different to the service for patients with solid tumours and has therefore been considered separately in parts of this analysis.

The Calman Hine report[16] proposed a structure for cancer services that would provide access to care as close to the patient's home as is compatible with high quality, safe and effective treatment. The structure was based on a network of expertise in cancer care reaching from primary care through cancer units in district general hospitals to cancer centres.

Following the publication of this report, cancer networks were established within the NHS. Each network has one or more cancer centre and several cancer units. In this study NCEPOD asked each hospital where SACT was administered to complete a separate organisational questionnaire. The information gathered reflects the facilities immediately available at each institution rather than the global resources of the trust.

The organisation

Type of hospital

In the organisational questionnaire it was asked whether the hospital was a cancer centre or cancer unit according to accepted definitions (Appendix 1). This information was cross checked by NCEPOD staff and adjusted as necessary.

The classification of hospitals into cancer centres and cancer units is not as simple as it first seems. There is no centrally held list of cancer centres and units. The Joint Collegiate Council for Oncology (JCCO) recognises three subtypes of cancer units, but they have not been distinguished between in this report; in part because not all hospitals were clear as to how they should be categorised.

Additionally, the NHS is constantly undergoing re-organisation. Services move between hospitals and occasionally trusts merge. For example, since starting this study at least one cancer centre that formed part of a trust has relocated from a stand alone site to a new wing of a large teaching hospital within the same trust.

Number of Hospitals

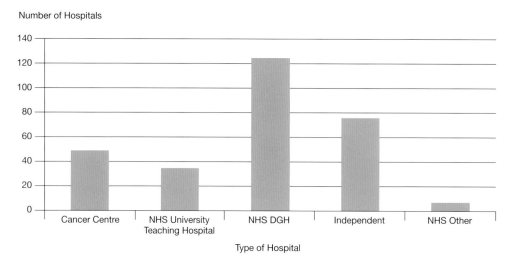

Type of Hospital

Figure 3.1. Distribution of organisations that took part in this study

Within this report only NHS hospitals with radiotherapy facilities have been classified as cancer centres (50). The other NHS hospitals where SACT was administered have been subdivided into NHS teaching hospitals (33), NHS district general hospitals (125) and NHS 'other' hospitals (9) – these were small community hospitals. Independent hospitals were considered separately (Figure 3.1).

Organisational facilities

Data from the 295 organisational questionnaires were analysed to identify the staff available to treat and care for cancer patients.

Staffing levels

STANDARD – haematological malignancies
There should be a rota for the facility which fulfils the following:
* Is staffed wholly by named consultants.
* Provides 24/7 cover for medical advice and/or presence in the facility when required.
* Has a minimum of 3 consultants on the rota.
* Each of the consultants is a core member of a haematology MDT and provides inpatient care for the facility as part of their timetable during normal working hours.
Manual for Cancer Services: Department of Health 2004[1] 3C-414

Table 3.1 shows the range of whole time equivalent (WTE) consultants in oncology specialties.

Table 3.1 Number of WTE oncology staff

WTE	Medical oncology (%)	Clinical oncology (%)	Haemato-oncology (%)	Palliative care (%)
< 1	72 (52)	83 (47)	32 (16)	81 (52)
1.0	17 (12)	11 (6)	23 (11)	43 (28)
>1 ≤ 2	13 (9)	19 (11)	48 (24)	23 (15)
>2 ≤ 3	12 (9)	12 (7)	46 (23)	8 (5)
>3 ≤ 4	3 (2)	6 (3)	20 (10)	1 (<1)
>4 ≤ 5	3 (2)	4 (2)	16 (8)	0
>5 ≤ 6	8 (6)	6 (3)	9 (4)	0
>6 ≤ 7	3 (2)	7 (4)	4 (2)	0
>7 ≤ 8	5 (4)	6 (3)	3 (1)	0
>8	3 (2)	22 (13)	1 (<1)	0
Subtotal	139	176	202	156
Unknown	33	29	24	24
Not answered*	123	90	69	115
Total	295	295	295	295

This question did not allow a 'no consultant' answer which may be reflected by the high number of 'not answered'.

Table 3.2 WTE Consultants in medical oncology (MO), clinical oncology (CO), haemato-oncology (HO) and palliative medicine (PM) by hospital type

	Cancer Centre				NHSUni TeachHosp				NHSDist GenHosp				Independent				NHS Other			
WTE	MO	CO	HO	PM	MO	CO	HO	PM	MO	CO	HO	PM	MO	CO	HO	PM	MO	CO	HO	PM
< 1	5	0	2	12	4	11	4	11	48	55	10	55	11	15	13	2	4	2	3	1
1.0	9	0	0	11	1	1	3	8	5	9	18	23	2	1	1	1	0	0	1	0
>1 ≤ 2	3	1	6	10	2	2	6	5	6	12	35	8	2	3	1	0	0	1	0	0
>2 ≤ 3	6	3	4	5	1	1	8	2	2	6	34	1	3	2	0	0	0	0	0	0
>3 ≤ 4	3	3	10	1	0	0	2	0	0	3	8	0	0	0	0	0	0	0	0	0
>4 ≤ 5	2	3	10	0	1	0	3	0	0	1	3	0	0	0	0	0	0	0	0	0
>5 ≤ 6	6	6	6	0	2	0	1	0	0	0	2	0	0	0	0	0	0	0	0	0
>6 ≤ 7	2	6	3	0	1	0	1	0	0	1	0	0	0	0	0	0	0	0	0	0
>7 ≤ 8	5	5	2	0	0	0	1	0	0	1	0	0	0	0	0	0	0	0	0	0
>8	3	21	1	0	0	0	0	0	0	1	0	0	0	0	0	0	0	0	0	0
Subtotal	44	48	44	39	12	15	29	26	61	89	110	87	18	21	15	3	4	3	4	1
Unknown	1	1	1	2	2	3	0	1	8	7	3	7	22	18	20	15	0	0	0	0
Not answered	5	1	5	9	19	15	4	6	56	29	12	31	38	39	43	60	5	6	5	8
Total	50	50	50	50	33	33	33	33	125	125	125	125	78	78	78	78	9	9	9	9

Table 3.2 shows the number of WTE consultants by hospital type. It can be seen that clinical and medical oncology consultants were primarily based in the cancer centres and teaching hospitals. A substantial number of hospitals where SACT was administered did so without the benefit of consultant oncologists and/or haemato-oncologists on site for more than a few sessions per week. While this is common practice in the independent sector it was also a feature of some NHS hospitals. Of the 295 hospitals that returned an organisational questionnaire 72 had sessions adding up to less than one full time consultant in medical oncology and 83 had less than one full time consultant clinical oncologist.

These figures may reflect the drive to provide services to patients nearer their homes. Haemato-oncological services were better represented in the district general hospitals than the other oncology specialties.

Table 3.3 shows that twenty five hospitals had less than one specialist chemotherapy nurse, and 19 had less than the equivalent of one full time specialist palliative care nurse. Furthermore, 183 hospitals had tumour site specific nurse specialists but we cannot be certain that they were in addition to the chemotherapy specialist nurses.

Table 3.3 WTE Specialist nurses

	Specialist nurses		
WTE	Chemotherapy (%)	Palliative care (%)	Tumour site (%)
< 1	25 (11)	19 (10)	8 (4)
.0	32 (14)	28 (14)	13 (7)
1 ≤ 2	46 (19)	69 (35)	16 (9)
2 ≤ 3	25 (11)	46 (23)	11 (6)
3 ≤ 4	21 (9)	20 (10)	13 (7)
4 ≤ 5	17 (7)	6 (3)	6 (3)
5 ≤ 6	17 (7)	5 (2)	9 (5)
6 ≤ 7	5 (2)	4 (2)	19 (10)
7 ≤ 8	9 (4)	0	16 (9)
8 ≤ 9	5 (2)	0	7 (4)
9 ≤ 10	4 (2)	1 (<1)	14 (8)
10	31 (13)	1 (<1)	51 (28)
Subtotal	237	199	183
Unknown	8	17	25
Not answered	50	79	87
Total	295	295	295

Emergency admissions

Of the 659 cases for whom a completed questionnaire B was returned, 557 patients were admitted to hospital during their last 30 days of life, of which 84 (15%) were admitted to a hospital other than the one in which their SACT was given.

Table 3.4 shows that the emergency admissions procedures and policies were different in the NHS compared to the independent sector.

It was noted that two cancer centres and four district general hospitals reported that there were no facilities for emergency admissions. The advisors considered that this might be a reflection of attention to detail by the person completing the questionnaire. Six NHS other hospitals, community hospitals, had no emergency admission service. Each hospital delivering SACT needs a clear emergency admissions policy for patients who develop complications. If admission is not directly to a ward with staff who are used to managing these patients it is particularly important that the staff that do assess and admit these patients are trained in their management.

Table 3.4 Emergency admissions facilities available in different types of hospital

| | Emergency admissions | | | | | | |
	24 hour ED or Direct to ward	24 hour ED	Direct to ward	No facility	Subtotal	Not answered	Total
Cancer Centre	25	11	12	2	50	0	50
NHSUniTeachHosp	17	12	4	0	33	0	33
NHSDistGenHosp	64	51	4	4	123	2	125
Independent	2	1	55	16	74	4	78
NHSOther	1	0	1	6	8	1	9
Total	109	75	76	28	288	7	295

The majority (109) of NHS hospitals that participated in this study had the infrastructure to admit emergency patients via the emergency department (ED) or directly to a ward. A small number (12) of NHS hospitals did not appear to accept emergency admissions. This included two cancer centres. A further 21 NHS hospitals specified that patients admitted with complications after SACT would go straight to a ward, but in 75 organisations patients would always be admitted through an ED. Patients at the majority of independent hospitals went directly to a ward as would be expected, but 16 hospitals indicated that they had no facility to receive emergency admissions.

Oncology staff available on call

Table 3.5 Consultant in medical/clinical oncology

	Resident	Non-resident	Unknown	Subtotal	Not answered	Total
Cancer Centre	1	43	3	47	3	50
NHSUniTeachHosp	0	14	3	17	16	33
NHSDistGenHosp	1	36	10	47	78	125
Independent	0	61	9	70	8	78
NHSOther	0	0	0	0	9	9
Total	2	154	25	181	114	295

Table 3.6 SpR/ST3+ in medical/clinical oncology

	Resident	Non-resident	Unknown	Subtotal	Not answered	Total
Cancer Centre	2	39	2	43	7	50
NHSUniTeachHosp	1	7	2	10	23	33
NHSDistGenHosp	5	9	7	21	104	125
Independent	3	2	0	5	73	78
NHSOther	0	0	0	0	9	9
Total	11	57	11	79	216	295

Table 3.7 SHO/ST1-2 in medical/clinical oncology

	Resident	Non-resident	Unknown	Subtotal	Not answered	Total
Cancer Centre	40	1	2	43	7	50
NHSUniTeachHosp	8	1	3	12	21	33
NHSDistGenHosp	9	2	7	18	107	125
Independent	12	1	0	13	65	78
NHSOther	0	0	0	0	9	9
Total	69	5	12	86	209	295

Table 3.8 F1/F2 in medical/clinical oncology

	Resident	Non-resident	Unknown	Subtotal	Not answered	Total
Cancer Centre	17	3	2	22	28	50
NHSUniTeachHosp	2	1	3	6	27	33
NHSDistGenHosp	9	4	8	21	104	125
Independent	0	1	0	1	77	78
NHSOther	0	0	0	0	9	9
Total	28	9	13	50	245	295

Table 3.9 Consultant in haemato-oncology

	Resident	Non-resident	Unknown	Subtotal	Not answered	Total
Cancer Centre	0	38	2	40	10	50
NHSUniTeachHosp	1	25	4	30	3	33
NHSDistGenHosp	11	85	13	109	16	125
Independent	0	44	1	45	33	78
NHSOther	0	0	1	0	8	9
Total	12	192	21	224	70	295

Table 3.10 SpR/ST3+ in haemato-oncology

	Resident	Non-resident	Unknown	Subtotal	Not answered	Total
Cancer Centre	2	27	3	32	18	50
NHSUniTeachHosp	1	18	4	23	10	33
NHSDistGenHosp	10	29	8	47	78	125
Independent	2	1	0	3	75	78
NHSOther	0	0	0	0	9	9
Total	15	75	15	105	190	295

Table 3.11 SHO/ST1-2 in haemato-oncology

	Resident	Non-resident	Unknown	Subtotal	Not answered	Total
Cancer Centre	30	1	1	32	18	50
NHSUniTeachHosp	16	1	3	20	13	33
NHSDistGenHosp	16	10	4	30	95	125
Independent	4	0	1	5	73	78
NHSOther	0	0	0	0	9	9
Total	66	12	9	87	208	295

Table 3.12 F1/F2 in haemato-oncology

	Resident	Non-resident	Unknown	Subtotal	Not answered	Total
Cancer Centre	14	3	2	19	31	50
NHSUniTeachHosp	5	1	3	9	24	33
NHSDistGenHosp	13	5	8	26	99	125
Independent	0	0	0	0	78	78
NHSOther	0	0	0	0	9	9
Total	32	9	13	54	241	295

General medical staff available on call

Table 3.13 Consultant in general medicine

	Resident	Non-resident	Unknown	Subtotal	Not answered	Total
Cancer Centre	2	27	3	32	18	50
NHSUniTeachHosp	1	17	4	22	11	33
NHSDistGenHosp	13	79	15	107	18	125
Independent	0	59	8	67	11	78
NHSOther	0	0	1	1	8	9
Total	16	182	30	229	66	295

Table 3.14 SpR/ST3+ in general medicine

	Resident	Non-resident	Unknown	Subtotal	Not answered	Total
Cancer Centre	23	4	5	32	18	50
NHSUniTeachHosp	17	1	4	22	11	33
NHSDistGenHosp	67	12	14	93	32	125
Independent	4	0	1	5	73	78
NHSOther	1	0	0	1	8	9
Total	112	17	24	153	142	295

Table 3.15 SHO/ST1-2 in general medicine

	Resident	Non-resident	Unknown	Subtotal	Not answered	Total
Cancer Centre	29	4	0	33	17	50
NHSUniTeachHosp	19	0	4	23	10	33
NHSDistGenHosp	72	7	16	95	30	125
Independent	15	0	1	16	62	78
NHSOther	0	0	0	0	9	9
Total	135	11	21	167	128	295

Table 3.16 F1/F2 in general medicine

	Resident	Non-resident	Unknown	Subtotal	Not answered	Total
Cancer Centre	21	2	4	27	23	50
NHSUniTeachHosp	16	0	5	21	12	33
NHSDistGenHosp	64	8	14	86	39	125
Independent	0	0	1	1	77	78
NHSOther	0	0	0	0	9	9
Total	101	10	24	135	160	295

Because so many hospitals did not provide information about on call cover it was difficult to determine how good or bad the availability of specialist advice was. However, from Tables 3.5 to 3.16 it can be seen that very few hospitals had clinical or medical oncologists above the grade of SHO/ST1-2 on call. There were more haemato-oncology SPR/ST3+ trainees on call although the majority of the on call cover on site remained with the very junior grades. In contrast, 107/148 NHS hospitals had an SPR/ST3+ resident on call for general medicine. It is clear that patients with complications of SACT who were admitted out of hours were more likely to be assessed and managed initially by a general medical trainee than by a trainee in oncology or haemato-oncology. In hospitals where there are too few oncology/haemato-oncology consultants to provide on call cover, the juniors will be supervised by a consultant from another medical specialty who may have very little experience of the management of patients with complications of SACT.

Facilities for the investigation of patients admitted with complications of SACT

When a patient receiving SACT becomes acutely unwell and is admitted to hospital the clinician will require easy access to basic radiological and laboratory investigations. Delays in requesting, performing, obtaining and therefore acting upon the results of essential investigations can lead to sub-optimal management of the patient. Each organisation was asked to provide information on the radiology and laboratory services available to them. Not all organisations provided data on all services and therefore the denominators for each facility vary.

Radiology services
Of the hospitals that provided an answer to this question 262 were able to get plain films 24 hours a day (Table 3.17). A further 20 hospitals had a restricted service.

Table 3.17 Plain films on site

Plain films on site					
	24 hours	Restricted hours	Subtotal	Not answered	Total
Cancer Centre	44	4	48	2	50
NHSUniTeachHosp	30	0	30	3	33
NHSDistGenHosp	115	7	122	3	125
Independent	72	4	76	2	78
NHSOther	1	5	6	3	9
Total	262	20	282	13	295

Ultrasound was available 24 hours per day in 197/254 hospitals that provided data (Table 3.18) with a similar number able to obtain CT scans (191/253) (Table 3.19) but, as would be expected, MRI scans were less commonly available. Indeed, access to such scans was poor in many hospitals (Table 3.20).

Table 3.18 Ultrasound on site

	Ultrasound on site				
	24 hours	Restricted hours	Subtotal	Not answered	Total
Cancer Centre	35	11	46	4	50
NHSUniTeachHosp	29	2	31	2	33
NHSDistGenHosp	82	24	106	19	125
Independent	50	17	67	11	78
NHSOther	1	3	4	5	9
Total	197	57	254	41	295

Table 3.19 CT on site

	CT scans on site				
	24 hours	Restricted hours	Subtotal	Not answered	Total
Cancer Centre	42	7	49	1	50
NHSUniTeachHosp	29	3	32	1	33
NHSDistGenHosp	100	15	115	10	125
Independent	20	36	56	22	78
NHSOther	0	1	1	8	9
Total	191	62	253	42	295

Table 3.20 MRI on site

	MRI scans on site				
	24 hours	Restricted hours	Subtotal	Not answered	Total
Cancer Centre	21	27	48	2	50
NHSUniTeachHosp	15	16	31	2	33
NHSDistGenHosp	41	63	104	21	125
Independent	14	51	65	13	78
NHSOther	0	1	1	8	9
Total	91	158	249	46	295

Laboratory services

STANDARD

Consultant microbiological advice must be available at all times.

There must be ready access to specialist laboratory facilities for the diagnosis of fungal or other opportunistic pathogens.

- A consultant clinical oncologist must be available for consultation, although radiotherapy facilities need not be on site.

Improving outcomes in haematological cancers: NICE 2003[6]

Most (262/288) hospitals had 24 hour access to haematology (Table 3.21). Of these, 224/228 were able to obtain results in under 4 hours and 163 in under one hour (Table 3.22).

Table 3.21 Access to haematology

		Access to haematology			
	24 hours	Restricted hours	Subtotal	Not answered	Total
Cancer Centre	48	2	50	0	50
NHSUniTeachHosp	30	0	30	3	33
NHSDistGenHosp	116	7	123	2	12
Independent	65	12	77	1	78
NHSOther	3	5	8	1	9
Total	262	26	288	7	295

Table 3.22 Time to obtain haematology results

Time for results	Number of hospitals (%)
1hr	163 (72)
1 - 4hrs	61 (27)
- 24hrs	4 (1)
Subtotal	228
Unknown	6
Not answered	61
Total	295

Table 3.23 Access to biochemistry

		Access to biochemistry			
	24 hours	Restricted hours	Subtotal	Not answered	Total
Cancer Centre	47	3	50	0	50
NHSUniTeachHosp	30	0	30	3	33
NHSDistGenHosp	116	6	122	3	125
Independent	65	12	77	1	78
NHSOther	3	5	8	1	9
Total	261	26	287	8	295

Table 3.24 Time to obtain biochemistry results

Time for results	Number of hospitals (%)
<1hr	129 (59)
1 - 4hrs	84 (38)
4 - 24hrs	7 (3)
Subtotal	220
Unknown	8
Not answered	67
Total	295

Also 261/287 hospitals had 24 hour access to biochemistry (Table 3.23), with 213/220 able to obtain results within 4 hours and 129 in less than one hour (Table 3.24).

Very few hospitals that had haematology and biochemistry facilities, could not have results in less than 4 hours. In those that could not, the majority were independent hospitals or NHSOther - e.g. community hospitals. However, one was a cancer centre and one a DGH. Certainly the lack of this facility in the cancer centre is not acceptable. There is a danger that treatment of complications of SACT will be delayed, or unnecessary treatment started, while the medical team awaits results.

Access to bacteriology was more restricted with only 211/276 hospitals having access 24 hours (Table 3.25). While culture and assessment of sensitivities can take more than 24 hours, microscopy of specimens such as urine or sputum may be valuable in the assessment of patients with pyrexia. In the absence of microscopy and sensitivities it will be necessary to start "best guess" antibiotics in the sick patient with sepsis.

Table 3.25 Access to bacteriology

	Access to bacteriology				
	24 hour	Restricted hours	Subtotal	Not answered	Total
Cancer Centre	41	6	47	3	50
NHSUniTeachHosp	27	2	29	4	33
NHSDistGenHosp	88	32	120	5	125
Independent	54	19	73	5	78
NHSOther	1	6	7	2	9
Total	211	65	276	19	295

Table 3.26 Time to obtain bacteriology results

Time for results	Number of hospitals (%)
<1hr	31 (18)
1 - 4hrs	49 (28)
4 - 24hrs	32 (19)
> 24hrs	60 (35)
Subtotal	172
Unknown	33
Not answered	90
Total	295

The provision of access to emergency radiology and laboratory services is important for the optimum care of patients who have complications of SACT, particularly neutropenic sepsis. Such care is compromised in those hospitals that cannot obtain necessary radiology and laboratory results in a timely manner. Some hospitals clearly recognise this and as described earlier did not accept emergency admissions. The disadvantage is that patients are then admitted to a hospital where they did not receive their SACT and this means that there will not be easy access to their casenotes and history.

Other specialties on site

Table 3.27 Availability of a general medical service

	Emergency general medical service					
	On site	Off site formal arrangement	Off site no formal arrangement	Subtotal	Not answered	Total
Cancer Centre	38	10	2	50	0	50
NHSUniTeachHosp	30	0	0	30	3	33
NHSDistGenHosp	121	3	1	125	0	125
Independent	51	9	13	73	5	78
NHSOther	0	7	1	8	1	9
Total	240	29	17	286	9	295

Table 3.28 Availability of a general surgical service

	\multicolumn{6}{c}{**Emergency general surgical service**}
	On site	**Off site formal arrangement**	**Off site no formal arrangement**	**Subtotal**	**Not answered**	**Total**
Cancer Centre	39	8	3	50	0	50
NHSUniTeachHosp	29	1	0	30	3	33
NHSDistGenHosp	117	7	1	125	0	125
Independent	52	12	7	71	7	78
NHSOther	0	6	1	7	2	9
Total	237	34	12	283	12	295

Experienced oncologists and haemato-oncologists are the best clinicians to manage patients with complications of SACT. However in the current system, as will be seen later in the report, a large proportion of patients admitted as emergencies are admitted under the care of general physicians. Conversely, there will be times when a patient admitted under the care of an oncologist or haemato-oncologist will require support from other specialties. Two of the specialties most likely to be called upon for an opinion are general medicine and general surgery. From the organisational data it could be seen that 240/286 hospitals had emergency general medicine on site (9/295 did not answer Table 3.27). Seventeen hospitals without emergency general medicine on site had no formal arrangement for access to a general medicine opinion, 13 of which were independent hospitals. The picture for emergency general surgery was similar with 237/283 hospitals having access to an emergency general surgery opinion on site (12/295 did not answer, Table 3.28). Seven of the twelve hospitals that had no general surgery on site and no formal arrangement for such an opinion were independent.

Resuscitation teams

Hospital trusts are required to have resuscitation policies in place[17]. This is essential in hospitals that admit emergency admissions. It was reported that 11 hospitals did not have a resuscitation team on site (an additional six hospitals did not answer this question). The hospitals without resuscitation teams included one cancer centre, three NHS DGHs, one independent and six NHS community hospitals. It is not appropriate that patients should be treated with parenterally administered SACT in a hospital without a resuscitation team unless the risk of an adverse event for a particular patient and particular regimen is very low. The trend is moving towards delivering SACT close to patients' homes e.g. in cottage hospitals, within the patient's home, or with a mobile chemotherapy bus service. Selected regimens and properly trained chemotherapy nurses who have received appropriate resuscitation training can make this feasible. However, adverse events occurring in patients treated with SACT in poorly equipped hospitals and also at home should be monitored and discussed within morbidity and mortality meetings at the centres responsible for devolving care.

Palliative care

The SACT prescribed for patients in this study was given with palliative intent in 557/649 (86%) cases (eight not answered). In the last weeks or days of life a palliative care team can help ensure optimal management of any symptoms causing distress to the patient. Seventy seven hospitals did not have a palliative care team on site (eight unanswered). Of the 156 hospitals that answered the question, 81 (52%) had palliative care consultant sessions adding up to less than one full time post (Table 3.1). There were however more palliative care nurses as only 19/199 (10%) hospitals had less than the equivalent of one full time post (Table 3.3).

Critical care beds (HDU, ICU, and ITU)

(see Appendix 1 for definitions)

Patients who become unwell after administration of SACT can become critically ill very rapidly. Such patients may benefit from the high ratio of nurse/patient staffing and close monitoring available in a critical care unit. Critical care consultants are involved in the care of patients admitted to Level 3 beds (ICU) and are available for advice when patients are in Level 2 beds (HDU).

Table 3.29 Distribution of Level 3 beds by hospital type

Level 3 (ICU) beds on site					
Type	Yes	No	Subtotal	Not answered	Total
Cancer Centre	40	9	49	1	50
NHSUniTeachHosp	31	0	31	2	33
NHSDistGenHosp	117	8	125	0	125
Independent	16	62	78	0	78
NHSOther	0	8	8	1	9
Total	204	87	291	4	295

Table 3.30 Distribution of Level 2 beds by hospital type

Level 2 beds (HDU) on site					
Type	Yes	No	Subtotal	Not answered	Total
Cancer Centre	37	12	49	1	50
NHSUniTeachHosp	31	1	32	1	33
NHSDistGenHosp	109	14	123	2	125
Independent	66	12	78	0	78
NHSOther	0	8	8	1	9
Total	243	47	290	5	295

Table 3.31 Formal arrangement for admission to Level 3 care for sites without Level 3 beds on site

	Formal arrangement				
Type	Yes	No	Subtotal	Not answered	Total
Cancer Centre	7	2	9	0	9
NHSUniTeachHosp	-	-	-	-	-
NHSDistGenHosp	8	0	8	0	8
Independent	55	2	57	5	62
NHSOther	6	2	8	0	8
Total	76	6	82	5	87

Of the hospitals in this study 204 had Level 3 beds (Table 3.29) and 243 had Level 2 beds (Table 3.30). All but six hospitals that did not have Level 3 critical care beds on site had a formal arrangement for admission of patients to another hospital when such beds were required (Table 3.31). This number reduced to only two hospitals without Level 3 beds that did not have a formal arrangement when hospitals with Level 2 beds were excluded from the analysis.

It is reassuring that hospitals without critical care facilities have established arrangements for the transfer of patients who need these facilities. As long as the need for critical care can be anticipated and transfers are made in a timely manner such arrangements are satisfactory. When such transfers are made it may be worthwhile discussing the circumstances in a morbidity and mortality meeting to consider how effective the process of transfer proved.

Key findings

84/557 (15%) patients admitted during the last 30 days of life were not admitted to the organisation where their SACT was administered.

17/286 hospitals where SACT was administered did not have a formal arrangement for access to general medical advice.

12/283 hospitals where SACT was administered did not have a formal arrangement for access to general surgical advice.

6/82 hospitals where SACT was administered that did not have on site Level 3 care had no formal arrangement with another hospital with regard to managing the acutely ill patient following treatment with SACT.

77 hospitals had no palliative care team on site and 81/156 (52%) hospitals had palliative care consultant sessions adding up to less than one full time post.

Recommendations

Hospitals admitting patients with complications of SACT that do not have emergency general medical and surgical services on site should have a formal arrangement with a hospital that can provide these services. *(Medical directors)*

Hospitals that treat patients with SACT but do not have the facilities to manage patients who are acutely unwell should have a formal agreement with another hospital for the admission or transfer of such patients as appropriate. *(Medical directors)*

A palliative care service should be available for all patients with malignant disease. *(Clinical directors)*

4 – Decision to treat

Introduction

The decision to treat a patient with systemic anti-cancer therapy (SACT) consists of a case review by the multidisciplinary team, a clinical assessment by the oncologist or haemato-oncologist and the patient's informed consent to treatment.

The multidisciplinary team should review the case history, pathology and radiological investigations, and after discussion of the treatment options, refer patients to the appropriate specialty for consideration of treatment.

The oncologist or haemato-oncologist should give advice on the most appropriate SACT regimen and assess whether the patient is fit enough for treatment. All possible clinical management plans should be discussed with the patient in a way that the patient can understand. This discussion should include the aims of treatment, its potential benefits and possible side effects, as well as the option of no treatment and information on the likely outcomes.

The patient should be given sufficient time to consider their decision regarding treatment and should receive supplementary information from other members of the multidisciplinary team.

The decision to treat is a combination of the doctor's decision to advise treatment and the patient's decision to accept the treatment offered. The decision making process is shared between the clinical team and the patient.

NCEPOD reviewed the cases of patients who died within 30 days of SACT in order to assess whether the decision to treat had been appropriate. Many patients died from progressive disease - the disease may have been too advanced for the patient to receive any benefit from the treatment offered. Some patients died as a direct result of the treatment given - these patients may have been too unwell for treatment.

Doctor's decision to offer treatment

SACT can be given as part of a clinical management plan in which the aim of treatment is cure of the malignancy or as part of a treatment aiming to control tumour growth, delay the onset of symptoms, prolong survival time or improve symptom control. The decision to treat a fit patient with a potentially curable malignancy, when there is a clear evidence base for the proposed treatment, is relatively straight forward. Difficulties arise when giving advice to patients with advanced end stage disease, who have already received a number of different courses of therapy and who may have co-morbidities.

Case study 1

History

A patient with advanced recurrent cancer was admitted with ascites, pleural effusions and a poor performance status. There had been evidence of bone marrow toxicity before the previous cycle of SACT but the chemotherapy doses had not been reduced. The patient had proven progressive disease and appeared in extremis. Nevertheless another course of SACT was recommended but the patient died the next day.

Problems noted by the advisors

- The last course of SACT should not have been given, and to recommend further SACT was futile
- The decision to treat appeared to have been influenced by the patient's young age and pressure from the family
- Palliative care would have been more appropriate but was not discussed.

The doctor's advice is based on both the tumour characteristics and the patient's medical fitness. Using information collated from the 657 completed questionnaires A, the following factors were analysed:

- tumour type;
- tumour stage;
- previous SACT treatment;
- medical complications of malignancy;
- patient's age;
- patient's performance status;
- patient's co-morbidities.

Tumour characteristics

Solid tumours

From Figure 4.1 it can be seen that the most common solid tumours (478) were lung (120), breast (82) and colorectal (79).

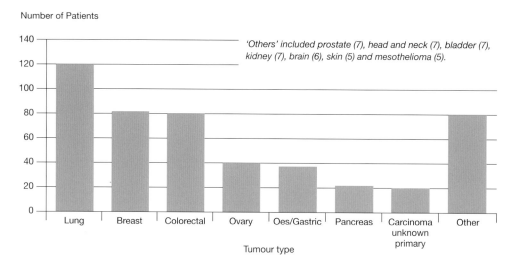

Number of Patients

'Others' included prostate (7), head and neck (7), bladder (7), kidney (7), brain (6), skin (5) and mesothelioma (5).

Tumour type

Figure 4.1 Frequency of solid tumours

Tumour stage of the 478 cases of solid tumours
Figure 4.2 shows that the majority of patients with solid tumours had advanced malignancy, 77% (354/458) had distant metastases and 15% (67/458) locally advanced disease with lymph node spread. In 37 (8%) patients the disease was limited to the primary site. Ten (2%) patients, had no evidence of disease at the time of SACT administration – these patients all received adjuvant chemotherapy.

20 not answered

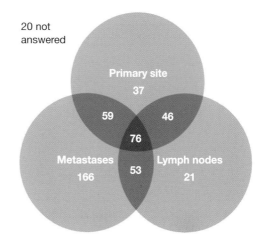

Figure 4.2 Known site(s) of disease prior to SACT course

Number of Patients

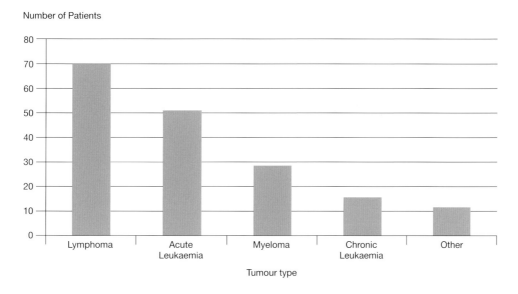

Tumour type

Figure 4.3 Frequency of haematological malignancies (179)

Haematological malignancies
From Figure 4.3 it can be seen that the most common haematological malignancies (179 cases) were lymphoma (69), acute leukaemia (52) and myeloma (28).

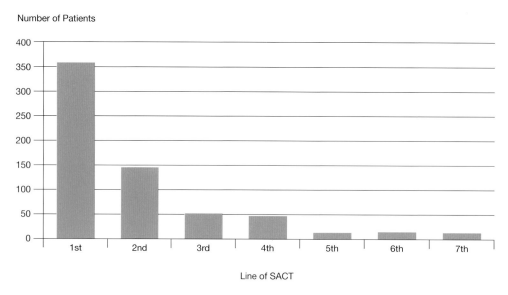

Number of Patients

Line of SACT

Figure 4.4 Line of treatment

Previous course/s of SACT

Patients with malignant disease may receive multiple courses of SACT during their treatment. Each course is referred to as a line of therapy. The initial treatment is 1st line, the second is 2nd line etcetera. With each line of therapy the likelihood of haematological toxicity increases and the probability of a positive response to treatment decreases. Figure 4.4 shows that 55% (362/657) of patients in this study group had received at least one previous course of SACT with some patients receiving 5th, 6th or 7th line treatment.

Examples of 7th line therapies

The following are examples of cases where 7 lines of therapy were administrated.

PR = partial response

SD = stable disease

PD = progressive disease

For details of tumour response criteria please see Appendix 4.

An example of breast cancer

Line of therapy	SACT Regimen	Response to treatment
Line 1	Cyclophosphamide, Methotrexate, 5 Fluorouracil	Adjuvant
Line 2	Cyclophosphamide, Adriamycin	PR
Line 3	Docetaxel	SD
Line 4	Capecitabine	PD
Line 5	Vinorelbine	PD
Line 6	Vinblastine, Methotrexate, Carboplatin	PD
Line 7	Cyclophosphamide, Methotrexate, 5 Fluorouracil	Unknown

An example of multiple myeloma

Line of therapy	SACT Regimen	Response to treatment
Line 1	Idarubicin, Dexamethasone	PD
Line 2	High dose Cyclophosphamide	PD
Line 3	Cyclophosphamide, Thalidomide, Dexamethasone	PR
Line 4	Etoposide, Methylprednisolone, Cytarabine, Cisplatin	SD
Line 5	Bortezomib, Dexamethasone	PR
Line 6	Cyclophosphamide, Thalidomide, Dexamethasone	Unknown
Line 7	Etoposide, Thalidomide	Unknown

Medical complications of malignancy

There were 394/657 (60%) patients who had a medical complication of their malignancy at the time the last course of SACT was delivered (shown in Figure 4.5 overleaf). These included hypoalbuminaemia (143 cases), pleural effusion (94 cases), ascites (72 cases), poor renal function (65 cases) and poor liver function (65 cases).

Number of Patients

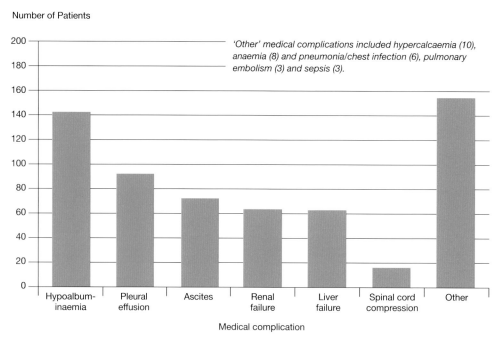

'Other' medical complications included hypercalcaemia (10), anaemia (8) and pneumonia/chest infection (6), pulmonary embolism (3) and sepsis (3).

Medical complication

Figure 4.5 Most common medical complications of the cancer

Patient factors

Age

The age range of the study group was 16-91 years with a median age of 65 years (Figure 4.6).

Number of Patients

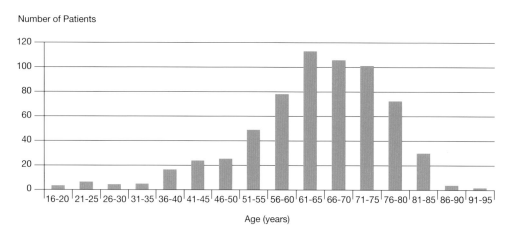

Age (years)

Figure 4.6 Age range of patients in the study

Performance status

Performance status was recorded using either the World
Health Organisation (WHO)/Eastern Co-operative
Oncology Group (ECOG) score or the Karnofsky
performance status scale (Tables 4.1 and 4.2).

Table 4.1 ECOG/WHO

0	Asymptomatic
1	Symptomatic but completely ambulant
2	Symptomatic, <50% in bed during the day
3	Symptomatic, >50% in bed, but not bed bound
4	Bed bound
5	Dead

Table 4.2 Karnofsky performance status scale definitions rating (%) criteria

100	Normal no complaints; no evidence of disease
90	Able to carry on normal activity; minor signs or symptoms of disease
80	Normal activity with effort; some signs or symptoms of disease
70	Cares for self; unable to carry out normal activity or to do active work
60	Requires occasional assistance, but is able to care for most of their personal needs
50	Requires considerable assistance and frequent medical care
40	Disabled; requires special care and assistance
30	Severely disabled; hospital admission is indicated although death not imminent
20	Very sick; hospital admission necessary; active supportive treatment necessary
10	Moribund; fatal processes progressing rapidly
0	Dead

The Karnofsky index was converted to the ECOG
grade to aid data analyses (Table 4.3).

Table 4.3 Conversion of Karnofsky scale to ECOG/Zubrod score

Karnofsky scale	ECOG score	Definition
90,100%	0	Fully active, able to carry out all pre-disease performance without restriction
70, 80%	1	Restricted in physically strenuous activity but ambulatory and able to carry out work of a light or sedentary nature
50, 60%	2	Ambulatory and capable of all self-care but unable to carry out any work activities. Up and about more than 50% of waking hours.
30.40%	3	Capable of only limited self-care, confined to bed or chair more than 50% of waking hours.
10, 20%	4	Completely disabled. Cannot carry on any self-care. Totally confined to bed or chair.
0%	5	Dead

From Figure 4.7 it can be seen that in 220/579 (38%) cases the patient had a performance status of 0 or 1 whereas in 235/579 (41%) cases the patient's performance status was 2 and in 122/579 (21%) it was low (3 or 4). The question was not answered in 78 cases.

Number of Patients

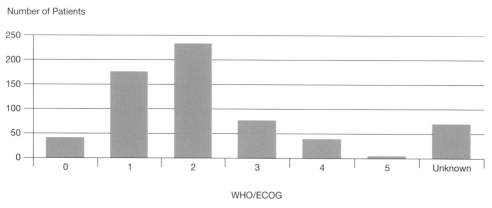

WHO/ECOG

Figure 4.7 Performance score of patients in the study

A performance status of 5 was recorded in 2 cases (5 = dead). This is a reflection of lack of care in completing the questionnaire, as a clear definition of the performance status grading was supplied.

A higher percentage of patients with haematological malignancies (37%) had a poor performance status (3 and 4) compared with the patients who had solid tumours (26%) (Figure 4.8).

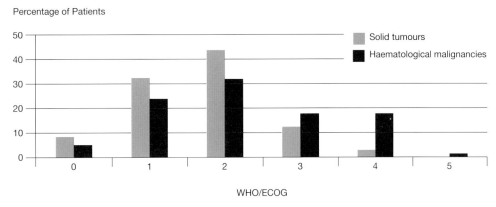

Figure 4.8 Performance score by type of cancer

The use of SACT in patients with a performance status of 4 is questionable. These patients are bed bound, incapable of any self care, completely disabled and in some cases moribund. However treatment may be justified if the patient has a very chemosensitive tumour which is potentially curable.

In the study group, 40 patients had a performance status of 4 immediately prior to commencement of the last course of SACT. The aim of treatment was cure of the malignancy in only 13/40 cases and high dose palliative in a further 7/40 cases (Table 4.4). Although the high dose palliative cases were not curable, long term disease control was thought possible with remissions lasting years.

The majority of cases with a performance status of 3 or 4 being treated with curative intent were patients with haematological malignancies (Table 4.5).

Table 4.4 Treatment intent in patients with a performance score of 4

Treatment intent	Number of patients
Potentially Curative	13
High Dose Palliative	7
Palliative	20
Total	40

Table 4.5 Treatment intent in patients with a performance score of 3 or 4 by type of cancer

Treatment intent	Solid tumours	Haematological malignancies	Total
Potentially Curative	3	17	20
High Dose Palliative	0	11	11
Palliative	62	29	91
Total	65	57	122

Case study 2

History

A middle-aged patient with a performance score (PS) 3 and liver metastases was planned to receive palliative chemotherapy. The consultant recommended that the starting dose should be 80% normal but this was not acted upon by the registrar who prescribed 100% doses. The patient suffered neutropenic sepsis following cycle one (neut 0.2) and was treated with GCSF, ciprofloxacin and fluconazole. The antibiotic was discontinued the day prior to the commencement of cycle two at which time WCC=20.2, neut =16.6. The drugs for cycle 2 were again prescribed at 100% doses.

Problems noted by the advisors

- Failure to adjust SACT dose in a patient with PS 3
- Failure to act on recommendation of consultant
- Administration of SACT in presence of active infection
- Failure to reduce dose of SACT following severe neutropenia with previous cycle.

Co-morbidities

Just over a third of the patients included in this study (37%; 245/657) were recorded as having co-morbidities - heart disease (94), diabetes mellitus (66), hypertension (45), lung disease (32), vascular disease (27) and renal disease (15) as defined by the consultant completing the questionnaire (Figure 4.9).

Patient population

In the collective opinion of the advisor group, the study population was similar to the total population receiving SACT in terms of age, tumour site and co-morbidities, but differed with regard to performance status, stage of disease, medical complications of malignancy and previous treatments. The study population had a relatively high percentage of poor performance status patients with advanced disease.

Number of Patients

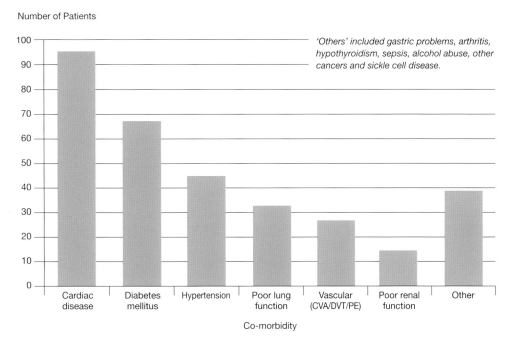

'Others' included gastric problems, arthritis, hypothyroidism, sepsis, alcohol abuse, other cancers and sickle cell disease.

Co-morbidity

Figure 4.9 Co-morbidities

The decision making process

STANDARD
The management of all cancer patients should be discussed at regular MDT meetings.
Manual for Cancer Services: Department of Health 2004[1]

NCEPOD looked at the decision making process in order to assess whether the decision to treat had been appropriate.

Tumour site specific multi disciplinary teams (MDTs) have been established in cancer centres and cancer units in order to improve the processes of care with better referral patterns, reduction in waiting times and adherence to local clinical care pathways. Cases are identified for discussion at regular MDT meetings following histological confirmation of malignancy. Most teams concentrate on tumour diagnosis, discuss the initial management plans and refer to an appropriate specialist for further assessment. However, cases may be discussed at a later date if a member of the MDT feels there is a point in the patient's management that requires discussion. In practice many patients may have more than one line of therapy – i.e. subsequent courses of SACT consisting of different combinations of drugs. Second or subsequent lines of therapy are not always discussed at an MDT because of time constraints and lack of resources.

MDT discussions

The most recent clinical management plan for a patient who died within 30 days of SACT was known to have been discussed at an MDT meeting in 58% (335/578) of cases. There was no discussion in 243 cases and in 79 cases it was unknown whether the case had been discussed.

Further analysis revealed that the percentage of cases discussed at a MDT meeting was associated with:

- service (oncology or haemato-oncology) (Table 4.6);
- primary tumour site (Table 4.7 and Table 4.8);
- treatment intent (Table 4.10);
- line of therapy (Table 4.11);
- age of the patient (Table 4.12);
- patient performance status (Table 4.13).

Table 4.6 Discussion at MDT by oncology or haemato-oncology service

	Course of SACT agreed at MDT				
	Yes (%)	No (%)	Subtotal	Not answered	Total
Haemato-oncology	113 (71)	46 (29)	159	20	179
Oncology	222 (53)	197 (47)	419	59	478
Total	335	243	578	79	657

Table 4.7 Discussion at MDT by primary tumour site - oncology cases

Type of cancer	Course of SACT agreed at MDT				
	Yes (%)	No (%)	Subtotal	Not answered	Total
Lung	67 (64)	38 (36)	105	15	120
Breast	19 (24)	59 (76)	78	4	82
Colorectal	43 (64)	24 (36)	67	12	79
Ovary	15 (52)	14 (48)	29	8	37
Oes/Gastric	24 (80)	6 (20)	30	3	33
Pancreas	14 (64)	8 (36)	22	2	24
Carcinoma unknown primary	10 (50)	10 (50)	20	3	23
Others	30 (44)	38 (56)	68	12	80
Total	222	197	419	59	478

Table 4.8 Discussion at MDT by type of haematological malignancy

	Course of SACT agreed at MDT				
Type of malignancy	Yes (%)	No (%)	Subtotal	Not answered	Total
Lymphoma	55 (81)	13 (19)	68	1	69
Acute leukaemia	29 (73)	11 (27)	40	12	52
Chronic leukaemia	8 (53)	7 (47)	15	2	17
Myeloma	17 (63)	10 (37)	27	1	28
Others	4 (44)	5 (56)	9	4	13
Total	113	46	159	20	179

Table 4.9 Treatment intent definitions

Neo-adjuvant	SACT prior to surgery and/or radiotherapy.
Adjuvant	SACT following surgery where tumour has been completely resected and there is no evidence of metastatic disease.
Potentially curative	SACT given with intent to cure.
High dose palliative	Where SACT is not necessarily curative but remissions can last years.
Palliative	SACT aimed at symptom control, quality of life improvement, tumour growth restraint or increased survival times.

Table 4.10 Discussion at MDT by treatment intent

	Course of SACT agreed at MDT				
	Yes (%)	No (%)	Subtotal	Not answered	Total
Neo-adjuvant	7 (88)	1 (12)	8	0	8
Adjuvant	9 (100)	0	9	1	10
Potentially curative	60 (88)	8 (12)	68	6	74
High dose palliative	14 (70)	6 (30)	20	0	20
Palliative	240 (51)	228 (49)	468	69	537
Subtotal	330	243	573	76	649
Not answered	5	0	5	3	8
Total	335	243	578	79	657

Table 4.11 Discussion at MDT by line of SACT

	Course of SACT agreed at MDT				
	Yes (%)	No (%)	Subtotal	Not answered	Total
First line SACT	121 (43)	158 (57)	279	33	312
Previous SACT	203 (73)	74 (27)	277	44	321
Subtotal	324	232	556	77	633
Not answered	11	11	22	2	24
Total	335	243	578	79	657

Table 4.12 Discussion at MDT meeting by age group

	Course of SACT agreed at MDT				
Age	Yes (%)	No (%)	Subtotal	Not answered	Total
6-40	17 (46)	20 (54)	37	5	42
41-65	137 (53)	120 (47)	257	38	295
> 65	181 (64)	103 (36)	284	36	320
Total	335	243	578	79	657

Table 4.13 Discussion at MDT meeting by performance status

	Course of SACT agreed at MDT				
Performance score	Yes (%)	No (%)	Subtotal	Not answered	Total
0	29 (73)	11 (27)	40	3	43
	107 (68)	51 (32)	158	19	177
	107 (51)	104 (49)	211	24	235
3	35 (45)	42 (55)	77	5	82
4	23 (64)	13 (36)	36	4	40
5	2 (100)	0	2	0	2
Subtotal	303	221	524	55	579
Unknown	32	22	54	24	78
Total	335	243	578	79	657

Potentially curative treatments were discussed more frequently than palliative therapies which would suggest that the MDT meetings concentrated mainly on first line therapies. However, data analysis based on line of therapy did not confirm this.

The cases more frequently discussed at an MDT meeting were:
- haematological malignancies (71%) compared with solid tumours (53%);
- upper gastro-intestinal tumours (80%) were discussed more frequently than breast cancers (24%);
- curative treatment intents (88%) compared with palliative care (51%);
- second or subsequent line therapy (73%) compared with first line therapy (43%);
- age group >65years (64%) compared with 16-40 years (46%);
- good performance status patients PS 0,1,2 (59%); compared with poor performance status patients PS 3,4,5 (52%).

The decision to initiate the most recent course of SACT was made by a consultant in 92% (593/647) of cases, and junior medical staff in 5% (34/647) of cases - non consultant career grade (NCCG) (20), specialist registrar (33), SHO (1). The grade of doctor was unknown in 10 cases (Table 4.14). However, when the SACT course had not been initiated by a consultant oncologist or haemato-oncologist (54 cases) 34 of them had been discussed at a MDT meeting.

Table 4.14 Decision to initiate a course of SACT
Initiator of course of SACT

Number of patients	(%)
Consultant	593 (92)
NCCG	20 (3)
SPR/ST3+	33 (5)
SHO/ST1-2	1 (<1)
Subtotal	647
Not answered	10
Total	657

The management plan

SACT course initiator

STANDARD
The service should agree and distribute a prescribing policy to the effect that:
The first cycle (at least) of a course of systemic chemotherapy should only be prescribed by a solid tumour oncologist or haemato-oncologist (as applicable) at consultant/specialist staff grade/SpR level, and for subsequent cycles, if not prescribed by one of the above, medical staff should ask advice of one of the above for changes of dose or cessation of therapy.
Manual for Cancer Services: Department of Health 2004[1] MC-150

Clinical care pathways

STANDARD
Oncologists should strive to establish uniform departmental policies for patients with defined types and stages of cancer. Keeping treatment variation to a minimum reduces the risk of error and facilitates the maintenance of high standards through audit of process and outcome. Common protocols and guidance should be used by cancer centres and cancer units.
Good Practice Guidance for Clinical Oncologists: Royal College of Radiologists[17]

A local written clinical care pathway was available for the management of the tumour type in 68% (446/657) of cases. This was followed in 95% (422/446) of patients. In the 24 cases where the local policy was not followed, the reasons given included poor patient performance status requiring a less toxic regimen, oral rather than intravenous therapy or in-patient rather than out-patient treatment. In two cases the patient was transferred from another centre and the SACT regimen already in use was continued, and in three cases the patient was treated with 3rd line therapy which was an exception to the local policy.

Treatment intent

The SACT regimen chosen is dependent on the tumour type, the extent of disease, the aims of therapy and previous treatments given.

Solid tumours

The fact that death occurred within 30 days of treatment was a particular cause for concern in the 35 patients where the aim of treatment was potentially curative, neo-adjuvant or adjuvant.

Table 4.15 shows that the treatment intent was palliative in 93% (441/476) of patients with solid tumours. Seventeen patients received potentially curative SACT, eight cases neo-adjuvant SACT prior to planned radical surgery and 10 cases adjuvant SACT following complete surgical excision of the tumour.

SACT regimens used

A list of regimens can be found in Appendix 2.

Figure 4.10 demonstrates that the more frequent combinations of SACT regimen and tumour type were:
- carboplatin and etoposide for lung cancer (32);
- oral capecitabine for colorectal cancer (17) or breast cancer (15);
- gemcitabine and carboplatin for lung cancer (29);
- oxaliplatin combinations for colorectal cancer (29);
- carboplatin for ovarian (15) cancer or lung (11) cancer (26);
- gemcitabine for pancreatic malignancies (19).

Table 4.15 Treatment intent by oncology service

	Oncology	Haemato-oncology
Treatment intent	Number of patients (%)	Number of patients (%)
Neo-adjuvant	8 (2)	0
Adjuvant	10 (2)	0
Potentially Curative	17 (4)	57 (33)
High Dose Palliative	0	18 (10)
Palliative	441 (93)	98 (57)
Subtotal	476	173
Not answered	2	6
Total	478	179

Number of Patients

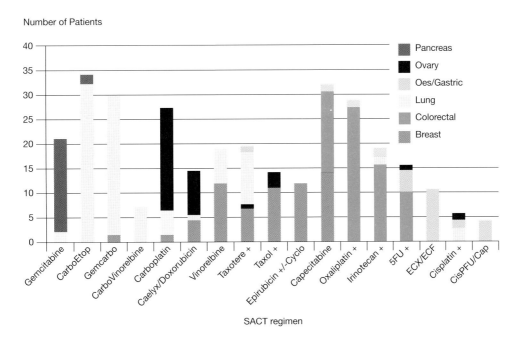

Figure 4.10 SACT regimens for solid tumours

Number of Patients

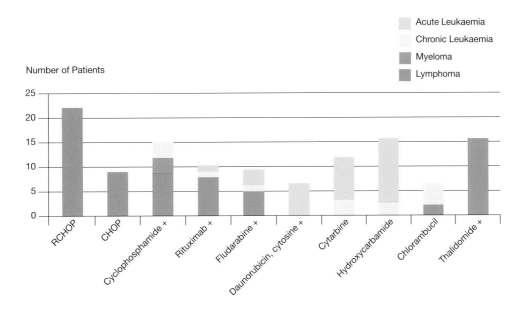

Figure 4.11 SACT regimens for haematology malignancies

Haematological malignancies

The treatment intent was palliative in 57% (98/173) of cases, potentially curative in 33% (57/173) and high dose palliative in 10% (18/173) of cases. Death within 30 days of treatment was of particular cause for concern in the 75 cases where chemotherapy was used for cure and high dose palliation.

Figure 4.11 shows that the more frequent combinations of SACT regimen and tumour type were:-

- R-CHOP (22) or CHOP (9) for non Hodgkin's lymphoma;
- Thalidomide combinations for myeloma (16);
- Hydroxycarbamide for end stage haematological malignancies (16).

Clinical trials

Whilst the majority of cancer management plans follow local clinical care pathways, some patients are entered into clinical trials where patient management is undertaken in accordance with the trial protocol. It was important to know whether patients included in this study had been recruited to a clinical trials. Patients in Phase I trials had been excluded from the study therefore the SACT was part of a clinical trial in just 4% (27/649) of cases; in eight cases it was unknown. Two cases were entered into single centre studies and 10 into multi-centre trials. Thirteen patients were entered into National Cancer Research Network approved trials and six patients into industry-sponsored studies.

Eighteen cases were solid tumours – including five colorectal cancers treated with oxaliplatin, capecitabine or cetuximab and three renal cell tumours treated with sunitinib or sorafenib.

Nine cases were haematological malignancies – of which five were acute leukaemias, two were myeloma and two were myelodysplasia.

All cancer centres had at least one research nurse (Table 4.16). The total numbers in each centre were variable with 55% (23/42) having 1- 5 nurses, 28% (12/42) having 6-10 nurses and 17% (7/42) more than 10 research nurses.

Table 4.16 shows that the research nurse levels within teaching hospitals and district general hospitals were lower with 16/17 of teaching hospitals and 91/92 of district general hospitals having five or less research nurses.

Patients decision to accept treatment: information and consent

Patient information

> **STANDARD**
> Many different healthcare professionals (doctors, radiographers, nurses, etc) are involved in an individual patient's treatment. It can be very confusing and disturbing for the patient to receive conflicting information and advice from different members of the same team caring for them. Good and consistent communication is, therefore, essential – not only between the team and the patient, but also between individual team members.
> **Making your chemotherapy service more patient-friendly: The Royal College of Radiologists 2008[19]**

In order to make an informed decision about whether to accept SACT or not, patients need access to relevant information about the potential risks and benefits of treatment in a form that they can understand. This information can be imparted in a number of ways. Tables 4.17 and 4.18 demonstrate how the organisations within this study reported that patient information was provided.

Table 4.16 Number of research staff employed by hospital type

WTE	Cancer Centre	NHSUniTeach Hosp	NHSDistGen Hosp	Independent	Other	Total
< 1	0	1	23	2	1	27
.0	2	6	28	0	0	36
> 1 ≤ 2	5	4	29	0	0	38
> 2 ≤ 3	5	3	8	0	0	16
> 3 ≤ 4	8	2	3	0	0	13
> 4 ≤ 5	3	0	0	0	0	3
> 5 ≤ 6	2	0	1	0	0	3
> 6 ≤ 7	3	0	0	0	0	3
> 7 ≤ 8	3	1	0	0	0	4
> 8 ≤ 9	1	0	0	0	0	1
> 9 ≤ 10	3	0	0	0	0	3
> 10	7	0	0	0	0	7
Subtotal	42	17	92	2	1	154
Unknown	3	3	7	11	0	24
Not answered	5	13	26	65	8	117
Total	50	33	125	78	9	295

Table 4.17 Information given to patients with solid tumours

Patient information given						
Type	Yes (%)	No (%)	Subtotal	Unknown	Not answered	Total
Verbal	262 (100)	0	262	2	31	295
Chemo leaflet	246 (98)	4 (2)	250	6	39	295
BACUP booklet	234 (95)	12 (5)	246	8	41	295
Chemo regimen leaflet	245 (99)	2 (1)	247	6	42	295
Audio visual info	122 (56)	96 (44)	218	21	56	295

Table 4.18 Information given to patients with haematological malignancies

	Patient information given					
Type	Yes (%)	No (%)	Subtotal	Unknown	Not answered	Total
Verbal	226 (99)	1 (<1)	**227**	4	64	**295**
Chemo leaflet	218 (99)	1 (<1)	**219**	8	68	**295**
BACUP booklet	212 (97)	6 (3)	**218**	10	67	**295**
Chemo regimen leaflet	217 (99)	1 (<1)	**218**	7	70	**295**
Audio visual info	101 (52)	92 (48)	**193**	17	85	**295**

It can be seen that in most hospitals, discussions about treatment were supplemented with leaflets and to a lesser degree, with audio visual information. There was no difference between the sub-specialties.

In addition to the organisational questionnaire the advisors were asked to assess the casenotes for evidence of information given to the patient. In 113 cases there was insufficient documentation to give a definite answer. However, in 314/ 433 (73%) of cases where it could be assessed there was documented evidence of information having been given to the patient.

Table 4.19 Information given to patients in the view of the advisors (answers may be multiple)

Verbal information by a doctor	287
Verbal information by a specialist nurse	58
Verbal information by another healthcare professional	6
Written information on SACT	118
Information on trial	19
DVD	2
BACUP booklet	45

Table 4.19 shows that in 287/314 (91%) cases the information was verbally given to the patient by a doctor and documented in the casenotes that this had happened. Written information was only documented as supplied in 118/314 (38%) cases and a BACUP booklet was documented as supplied in only 45 cases. Either less information is given than organisations believe or the giving of information is poorly documented. In eight cases the advisors found that the patient received conflicting information from different staff and in another nine cases the information was considered to be inaccurate.

In those cases where it was not documented whether information had been supplied it is not possible to know whether it was given or not. Recording the giving of information in the casenotes helps communication between team members and can reduce unnecessary duplication of information being provided to the patient as well as helping identify when further information should be given. NCEPOD noted that the contribution of specialist nurses to imparting information was often not recorded.

Previous NCEPOD reports[8,9] have highlighted poor note-keeping on hospital records and the effect that this can have on making it difficult to determine the standard of care the patient received.

Probability of benefit

For patients to understand the risks and benefits of the proposed treatment they need realistic estimates of the probability of benefit. The local clinicians completing questionnaire A were asked to estimate the probability of cure for each patient (Table 4.20), and also to indicate from a selection of choices which best described the treatment intent. Clinicians were provided with definitions of the terms used.

Table 4.20 Estimated chance of cure in the view of clinicians completing questionnaire A

Estimated chance of cure	Number of patients (%)
50%	16 (2)
20-49%	43 (7)
<20%	85 (13)
0%	497 (78)
Subtotal	641
Not answered	16
Total	657

During development of this study there was considerable discussion about the classification of treatment intent. Adjuvant and neo-adjuvant treatments were the easiest to define. 'High-dose palliative treatment' was a term more commonly used by haemato-oncologists. NCEPOD defined potentially curative as SACT given with the intent of cure. The clinicians returning questionnaire A indicated that SACT was given with neo-adjuvant, adjuvant or potentially curative intent in 92 cases, yet in only 16/641 cases was the probability of cure thought to be over 50% (Table 4.20).

Although SACT can improve prognosis or offer cure from a life-threatening cancer, treatment carries certain risks, including death as a direct consequence of treatment. Patients may have very strong, and sometimes unrealistic, views on the balance of risk and benefit in relation to SACT. It is the clinician's role to explain to a patient the likely risks and benefits to them as an individual.

Case study 3

History

A young patient with widespread cancer had progressive disease after several lines of SACT. The patient was seen by a palliative care doctor. At the patient's request a new line of treatment was commenced despite a performance score of 4. The probability of benefit was not recorded in the consent form or in the notes. The patient died within hours of receiving SACT.

Problems noted by the advisors

- The treatment with further SACT was futile and should not have been prescribed
- Palliative care teams should be prepared to question the decision to treat.

Consent

The most recent GMC guidance on consent emphasises the shared process by which the patient and doctor work together to reach a decision about whether or not the patient will accept treatment[20]. For consent to be valid, the patient must have been in a position to make a profoundly personal choice. In law that means that they must have the capacity, sufficient information and sufficient time to make a choice and give consent voluntarily. The doctor must put at the patient's disposal the information that they need, in a form that they can understand, so that the patient can make that choice.

Capacity

The law relating to decision-making and consent, particularly for patients who lack capacity, varies across the UK; doctors need to understand the law as it applies where they work. Guidance is available from the Department of Health[21].

Sufficient time to make a decision

Although patients may have access to a plethora of information published by cancer charities and patient support groups, this is no substitute for "bespoke" information tailored to fit the individual patient and their condition. Patients must be allowed their choice, but it is also the doctor's duty to avoid subjecting the patient to treatment which is clearly futile. This was highlighted in a recent study by Audrey *et al*[31] who reviewed information given to patients being offered palliative chemotherapy and found that most patients were not given clear information about potential survival benefits.

The process of consent may require more than one discussion to reflect the evolving nature of treatment. Patients must feel free to change their minds. There should always be an opportunity for patients to modify or withdraw consent about a decision at any time, or to request treatment previously declined as long as they are still likely to benefit. When there is a delay between consent and administration of SACT, a member of the healthcare team should check that the patient has no further concerns before treatment is administered.

Patients must be kept informed about the progress of their treatment, and be allowed the opportunity to make decisions at all stages of treatment, not just in the initial stage. If the treatment is ongoing there should be clear arrangements in place to review decisions and, if necessary, to make new ones.

STANDARD

However consent is obtained, written information should be provided concerning every chemotherapy protocol being used. This should contain detailed information, written in layman's terms, about:

(a) treatment intention

(b) expected response rates

(c) anticipated side effects including incidence of morbidity and mortality from neutropaenia

(d) duration of treatment - numbers of cycles of chemotherapy and length of time in hospital for each course

(e) possible late effects of chemotherapy including sterility and second malignancies

(f) necessity for blood product transfusion, administration of antibiotics and antifungal agents

Obtaining Consent for Chemotherapy: British Committee for Standards in Haematology Guidelines[21]

The consent form

While there is no legal requirement to obtain *written* consent for SACT, it is advisable. Consent forms help document the process of consent, although a signed consent form does not in itself confirm that consent is valid.

Grade of medical staff obtaining patients consent to treatment

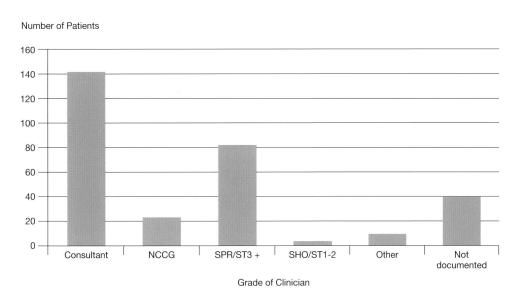

Figure 4.12 Grade of clinician taking consent

NCEPOD only received a consent form signed by the patient and a doctor in 310 of the 546 sets of casenotes received (Figure 4.12). The name and status of doctors taking consent should always be made clear on the consent form. In 44/310 cases it was not possible to determine the grade of the doctor. This is unacceptable. Where the grade of the doctor was clear, consent was usually taken by a consultant, staff grade or trainee doctor in the later years of training. There was considerable discussion amongst the advisors about whether junior staff receive sufficient training in obtaining consent from patients with a prognosis as poor as those seen in this study. The back of the consent form in general use in NHS hospitals carries clear guidelines on who can seek consent. NCEPOD considers it inappropriate that the consent form could be signed by doctors not considered competent to prescribe SACT.

Content of consent form

It was apparent from the consent forms reviewed that information that would be expected on the consent form is often missing. In only 27 cases was it recorded on the consent form that SACT could be life-threatening and of these in four cases the treatment intent was potentially curative. Although common toxicities were recorded on 234/310 (75%) consent forms, the most serious toxicities were only recorded on 160/310 (52%).

The advisors judged that the consent form should be completed with greater care and include the likelihood of common and serious toxicities, as well as the risk of death due to treatment. The likely improvement in survival against no treatment (or where appropriate the probability of cure) should also be included. The consent form should be signed by a clinician competent to prescribe SACT and the clinician should make their grade clear. The consent form in routine use in NHS hospitals has a space for the clinician to record their job title. This should be modified so the grade of the clinician is recorded and is unambiguous.

The appropriateness of the decision to treat

Some of the patients in this study were heavily pre-treated, had several co-morbidities, a poor performance status and advanced disease. They were therefore at an increased risk of treatment related toxicity and/or death from progressive disease compared to the total population seen in any chemotherapy clinic. Separate assessments of whether or not the decision to treat with the most recent course of SACT was appropriate were made by both the advisory group and the local oncologist.

Advisors' opinion on decision to treat with SACT

The advisors were able to reach a judgement in 513/546 cases.

Table 4.21 Advisors' view of the whether the most recent course of SACT was appropriate

Course appropriate (advisors' view)	Number of patients (%)
Yes	417 (81)
No	96 (19)
Subtotal	**513**
Unknown	33
Total	**546**

Table 4.21 shows that the advisors believed that the decision to treat was inappropriate in 19% (96/513) of cases. The reasons cited included:
- poor performance status (44);
- lack of evidence that further treatment would be of benefit (14);
- abnormal pre-treatment investigations (5);
- patients with end stage disease (5).

Where the decision to treat with SACT was considered by the advisors to be appropriate, 60% (211/349) had been discussed at an MDT meeting, compared to 48% (37/77) of cases, where the decision was considered to be inappropriate (Table 4.22).

Table 4.22 Appropriateness of SACT in the view of the advisors compared to whether the case had been discussed at a MDT meeting.

SACT appropriate (advisors' view)	Course of SACT agreed at MDT				
	Yes (%)	No (%)	Subtotal	Not answered	Total
Yes	211 (60)	138 (40)	349	48	397
No	37 (48)	40 (52)	77	9	86
Subtotal	248	178	426	57	483
Insufficient data	15	14	29	4	33
Total	263	192	455	61	516

* These data were taken from a combination of questionnaire A and the assessment form. In 30/546 cases questionnaire A was not completed.

Local clinician's opinion on decision to treat

In 18% (118/657) of cases, the local consultants completing clinical questionnaire A commented that the decision whether or not to treat a patient with advanced disease and a poor performance status was a difficult decision to make.

The local consultants believed, in retrospect, that the decision to treat may have been inappropriate in 13% (85/657) of patients. However, in 7% (46/657) of cases they believed that the patient, and the patient's relatives, had been fully informed of the possible toxicity and likely response rates and that not withstanding this, the patient had made an informed decision to undergo therapy. In 6% (38/657) of cases the consultant would have acted differently.

Both the advisor and the local oncologist deemed the decision to treat may have been inappropriate in one in five cases. However, there were differences in the overall opinion. The advisors made their judgement purely on the data presented and believed that in all of these cases the decision to treat was inappropriate. The local clinician admitted that the decision was difficult to make, but in retrospect believed that in two thirds of cases their action could be justified. The review by a local oncologist benefits from a more detailed knowledge of the individual patient. However, when faced with difficult decisions, the oncologist may benefit from a second opinion from a colleague or from further discussion with the multidisciplinary team.

Examples of clinicians' comments

MDT decision

"The treatment decision was difficult. An aggressive lymphoma, poor prognostic features, poor performance status. However we (MDT) believed it was reasonable to give full dose chemotherapy."

Consensus decision

"Seemed uncertain from the beginning whether the patient was fit enough for chemotherapy. There is no right or wrong here - only a consensus opinion between the medical team, the patient and the family."

Patient's decision

"Tragically a young patient with children who would not accept NO further treatment - we gave treatment at 50% doses in order to reduce the risk of toxicity but it also had very little chance of working either."

Difficult decision

"With the benefit of hindsight one would not treat this patient who died from progressive disease. Occasionally even advanced disease responds to second line chemotherapy and although in hindsight the correct decision may well be very clear, it is sadly not available at the time of the decision to treat".

Wrong decision

"I should not have given further chemotherapy to this patient. In retrospect this is a decision I regret. The patient was clearly dying. However the patient was lucid, well informed and asked if there was any chemotherapy that they hadn't tried. I should have explained that there wasn't. During the consent I explained that it was very unlikely that the chemotherapy would have any beneficial effect."

Key findings

86% (557/649) of patients in this study were treated with palliative intent.

14% (92/649) of patients in this study were treated with curative intent.

45% (295/657) of patients who died within 30 days of SACT were receiving second or subsequent line therapy.

21% (122/579) of patients who died within 30 days of SACT had a performance score of 3 or 4 at the time of the decision to commence the most recent course of SACT, i.e. severely debilitated.

In 19% (96/513) of cases the decision to treat with the most recent course of SACT was inappropriate in the advisors' view.

The clinical management plan was discussed at an MDT meeting in only 58% (335/578) of patients who died within 30 days of SACT.

In 14% (44/310) of cases the grade of doctor taking consent was not documented on the consent form.

In 25% (76/310) of cases common toxicity was not recorded on the consent form.

In 48% (150/310) of cases serious toxicity was not recorded on the consent form.

Recommendations

NCEPOD supports the Manual for Cancer Services standard that initial clinical management plans for *all* cancer patients should be formulated within a multidisciplinary team meeting. The MDT should be responsible for agreeing clinical care pathways, including appropriate chemotherapy regimens, doses and treatment durations. *(Clinical directors)*

The decision whether or not to advise SACT should be undertaken by a consultant oncologist/haemato-oncologist after a comprehensive clinical review of the patient. *(Clinical directors and consultants)*

The decision whether to accept treatment should be made by the patient after they have been fully informed of the potential benefits and toxicities and have had sufficient time to consider their decision and discuss it with their family and carers. *(Clinical directors)*

There should be greater standardisation of the consent form. The name and grade of doctor taking consent should always be stated on the consent form. *(Cancer services managers, clinical directors and medical directors)*

Consent must only be taken by a clinician sufficiently experienced to judge that the patient's decision has been made after consideration of the potential risks and benefits of the treatment, and that treatment is in the patient's best interest. *(Clinical directors)*

Giving palliative SACT to poor performance status patients grade 3 or 4 should be done so with caution and having been discussed at a MDT meeting. *(Consultants)*

5 – SACT prescriptions and administration

Introduction

The pre-treatment assessment, prescribing, dispensing and administration of systemic anti-cancer therapy (SACT) is undertaken by a large multidisciplinary team consisting of doctors, specialist chemotherapy nurses, cancer pharmacists and the laboratory services.

SACT is prepared within the pharmacy departments and administered by specialist nurses in designated units. As the SACT work load has increased, the roles of pharmacists and specialist nurses have been extended. Some have been trained as supplementary or independent prescribers; others provide patient education clinics and a telephone follow up service after SACT administration. Pharmacists are responsible for the production of the pre-printed prescriptions and maintenance of the electronic prescribing systems. The specialist nurses contribute to the production of the patients' information leaflets.

PRESCRIBING SACT

Authorisation to prescribe SACT

The prescribing of SACT is limited to appropriately trained staff. The decision to initiate a course of SACT is undertaken at consultant level or delegated to a competent SpR during periods of the consultant's leave. In contrast the prescribing of each cycle of treatment can be delegated to other grades of medical staff or independent or supplementary prescribers such as specialist chemotherapy nurses or cancer pharmacists.

STANDARDS

Chemotherapy must be initiated and supervised only by clinicians who are appropriately accredited and/or experienced.
Good Practice Guidance for Clinical Oncologists: Royal College of Radiologists[17]

The service should agree and distribute a prescribing policy to the effect that:
- The first cycle (at least) of a course of systemic chemotherapy should only be prescribed by a solid tumour oncologist or haemato-oncologist (as applicable) at consultant/specialist staff grade/SpR level.
- For subsequent cycles, if not prescribed by one of the above, medical staff should ask advice of one of the above for changes of dose or cessation of therapy.

Manual for Cancer Services: Department of Health 2004 3C-150[1]

Organisations which maintained a list of staff authorised to initiate and prescribe SACT

Table 5.1 Lists of SACT initiators and prescribers kept

	List maintained	
	Initiator (%)	Prescriber (%)
Yes	210 (77)	189 (71)
No	61 (23)	78 (29)
Subtotal	271	267
Unknown	11	13
Not answered	13	15
Total	295	295

Information from the 295 hospitals that completed the organisational questionnaire revealed that 77% (210/271) of centres maintained a list of doctors authorised to initiate SACT (no information submitted from 24 organisations) and 71% (189/267) had a list of clinicians permitted to prescribe second and subsequent cycles (no information submitted from 28 organisations, Table 5.1).

Of the 210 hospitals that kept a list of SACT initiators, 207 provided further details on staff grades.

Further analysis shown in Figure 5.1 demonstrated that consultants were authorised to initiate SACT in all 207 hospitals. In 63% (131/207) of hospitals consultants alone could initiate SACT. In addition to consultants, non consultant career grades could initiate SACT in 25% (52/207) of hospitals, specialist registrars in 23% (48/207) and SHOs were allowed to do this in 1% (3/207). It is not acceptable that SHOs are allowed to do this.

Initiators of a course of SACT

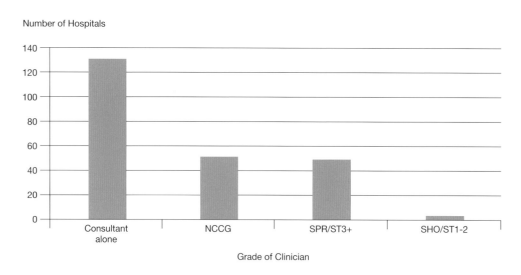

Figure 5.1 Grade of clinicians who were permitted to initiate SACT

Prescribers of cycles of SACT

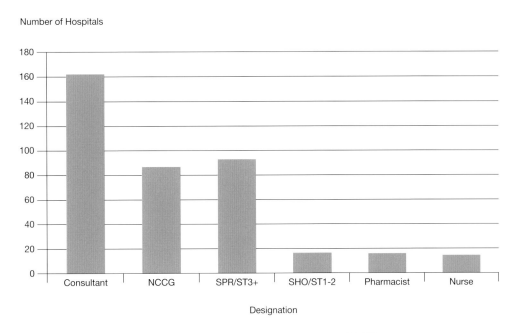

Number of Hospitals

Designation

Figure 5.2 Prescribers of cycles of SACT

Of the hospitals that maintained a list of SACT prescribers, 181/189 provided further details on staff grades.

NCEPOD advisors remarked on the fact that SHO/ST1/ST2 grades were authorised to prescribe SACT in 17 hospitals (Figure 5.2) and in three of these hospitals they were permitted to initiate the course of treatment which is not in line with the Royal College of Radiologists' – Good Practice Guidance for Clinical Oncologists standard[18].

Staff permitted to prescribe subsequent cycles of therapy included consultants in 90% (163/181) of hospitals, NCCG in 48% (86/181), SpR/ST3+ in 51% (93/181), SHO/ST1-2 in 9% (17/181) and supplementary prescribers in 18% (32/181) This list was limited to consultants only in 30% (55/181) of hospitals; however 37 of these were independent hospitals.

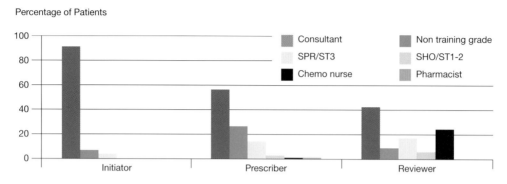

Percentage of Patients

Figure 5.3 Grade of staff initiating, prescribing and reviewing the prescriptions for SACT

Grade of staff initiating and prescribing the most recent cycle of SACT and reviewing the patient on day 1 of administration of SACT

Analysis of the data from questionnaire A revealed that the last course of SACT was initiated by a consultant in 92% (593/647) of cases (10 cases unknown), whilst the work of prescribing the last cycle of treatment was shared between consultant (57%; 356/630) and junior medical staff (43%;269/630). The member of staff reviewing the patient on the day of chemotherapy was usually a consultant (41%; 262/630), junior doctor (34%; 213/630) or a chemotherapy nurse (24%; 154/630) (Figure 5.3).

Training in SACT prescribing

Junior medical staff and independent prescribers receive specialist training in SACT prescribing, and in some hospitals are required to demonstrate their competency in SACT prescribing before being locally accredited and allowed to work unsupervised. They should have a workload appropriate to their level of expertise and follow written clinical protocols.

Tables 5.2 and 5.3 show that across all hospitals, training of junior doctors to prescribe SACT was low. When cancer centres were investigated alone it could be seen that more did provide training than did not, but it was still very low.

Table 5.2 Junior doctor training in medical/clinical oncology

	Training supplied for junior doctors in medical/clinical oncology				
	Yes(%)	No(%)	Subtotal	Not answered	Total
All hospitals	61 (26)	174 (74)	235	60	295
Cancer centres	33 (70)	14 (30)	47	3	50

Table 5.3 Junior doctor training in haemato-oncology

	Training supplied for junior doctors in haemato-oncology				
	Yes(%)	No(%)	Subtotal	Not answered	Total
All hospitals	57 (26)	165 (74)	222	73	295
Cancer centres	22 (56)	17 (44)	39	11	50

Table 5.4 When junior doctors can prescribe SACT

	Clinical/medical oncology	Haemato-oncology
Immediately upon employment	4	4
At the discretion of the consultant	54	57
Post formal assessment/accreditation	31	32
Subtotal	**89**	**93**
Unknown	63	58
Not answered	143	144
Total	**295**	**295**

However, this may be explained if centres/hospitals only treat solid/haematologial cancers and therefore do not need to provide training in prescribing for the other.

In addition to the training available, Table 5.4 shows that junior doctors underwent a formal assessment of competency, before being authorised to prescribe SACT, in only 32 organisations. Of particular note were four hospitals that allowed junior staff to start prescribing SACT immediately upon employment, whilst in 57 centres this was at the discretion of the consultant. No information was available from 206 centres (these hospitals may not have had junior oncologists).

Independent and supplementary prescribers

With the increasing workload in chemotherapy clinics, specialist nurses and pharmacists have been trained as independent or supplementary prescribers. At the time of this study supplementary prescribers were used in 26 oncology centres (10 nurses, 14 pharmacists, 2 nurses and pharmacists) and 19 haemato-oncology centres (11 nurses, 7 pharmacists, 1 nurse and pharmacist).

In total 32 organisations used supplementary prescribers in their oncology or haematology departments. The training undertaken included accreditation following a supplementary prescribers' course (23/32 centres) or local training and supervision by the consultant (6/32 centres). No information on training was received from three centres. The courses attended included the Royal Pharmaceutical Society (RPS) course, non medical prescribing (NMP) courses, and other courses for supplementary prescribers – such as the English National Board (ENB) for nurses and the Nursing and Midwifery Council (NMC-V300).

The work of supplementary prescribers in oncology departments included prescribing adjuvant chemotherapy for breast and colorectal cancer. Within haemato-oncology departments, a wide variety of the more commonly used regimens were prescribed. Written local protocols were available to follow in 22/26 of oncology departments and 17/19 of haemato-oncology departments.

NCEPOD was concerned that in some organisations the supplementary prescribers only received local training or supervision by the consultant rather than attendance at a formal course and accreditation.

ASSESSMENT PRIOR TO EACH CYCLE OF SACT

SACT is administered as a course of treatment consisting of a number of treatment cycles.

Before starting a course of SACT, patients undergo a clinical examination and blood tests to estimate the full blood count (FBC), liver function (LFT) and renal function (RFT). Additional investigations may be indicated depending on the SACT regimen used and the patient's co-morbidities.

STANDARDS
Renal function should be monitored during treatment and doses modified as appropriate if there is a significant change in renal function.
Chemotherapy Guidelines: COIN 2001 Grade B[2]

Patients should have their glomerular filtration rate (GFR) evaluated…before receiving potentially nephrotoxic cytotoxics or chemotherapy cleared primarily by the kidney.
Chemotherapy Guidelines: COIN 2001 Grade C[2]

Before each subsequent cycle of treatment the patient should be re-assessed for clinical performance status and treatment related toxicity from the previous cycle. The essential pre-treatment blood tests are repeated and SACT should be administered if the results of these investigations are within the acceptable range for the chemotherapy regimen used. The dose and timing of chemotherapy should be adjusted according to the patient's clinical condition and previous toxicity.

Tumour response to treatment is assessed at appropriate intervals dependent on the treatment intent and SACT regimen used.

STANDARDS
There should be treatment records for each patient fulfilling the following minimum criteria, prior to the start of a course of chemotherapy:
- Investigations necessary prior to starting the whole course.
- Investigations to be performed serially during the course (to detect/monitor both toxicity and response) and their intended frequency.
- For palliative, curative and neo-adjuvant treatments, i.e. any treatment other than adjuvant; the maximum number of cycles after which the response to treatment is to be reviewed prior to continuing the course.

Manual for Cancer Services: Department of Health 2004 3C-137[1]

There should be treatment records for each patient fulfilling the following minimum criteria, prior to each cycle.
- The results of essential serial investigations applicable to that cycle (and prior to an administration within a cycle, if applicable).
- Any dose modifications and whether or not they are intended to be permanent.
- Any cycle (or administration) delays.

Manual for Cancer Services: Department of Health 3C-138[1]

Sufficient documentation was available for the advisors to assess the pre-treatment investigations and clinical assessments in 84% (461/546) of cases.

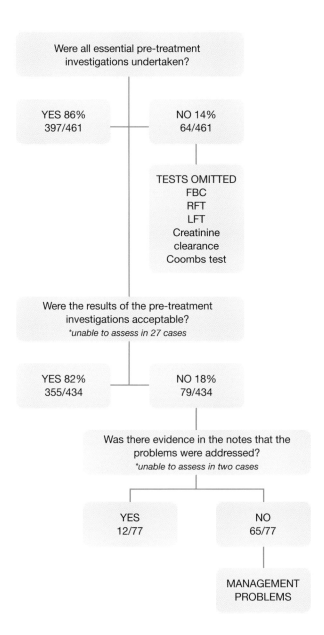

Figure 5.4 Advisors' opinion on the pre-treatment investigations

In the advisors' view all essential pre-treatment investigations had been undertaken in 86% (397/461) of cases (Figure 5.4). Essential investigations had been omitted in 14% (64/461) of cases and there were insufficient data to comment on 85 cases. The omitted investigations included full blood count (FBC) – 12 cases, renal function tests (RFT) - 17 cases, liver function tests (LFT) - 24 cases, creatinine clearance estimation - 9 cases receiving platinum drugs, a Coombs test in a patient receiving fludarabine and an echocardiogram in two patients receiving anthracycline.

Table 5.5 Acceptable pre-treatment investigations in the view of the advisors

Acceptable results	Number of patients (%)
Yes	355 (82)
No	79 (18)
Subtotal	**434**
Unknown	112
Total	**546**

In the view of the advisors the results of the pre-treatment investigations undertaken were acceptable in 82% (355/434) of cases where it could be assessed but unacceptable for full doses of SACT in 18% (79/434) cases. In 112 cases the investigation results were not available for review (Table 5.5).

The SACT regimen had been adjusted appropriately in 12/77 of cases with abnormal test results. There was insufficient evidence to comment on 2 cases. However, management was suboptimal in 65/77 of these cases.

Examples of poor management included:

- no investigation of elevated white cell count (WCC) – 8 cases – all these patients had solid tumours;
- no dose reduction despite neutropenia (2) – both solid tumours, thrombocytopenia (4) – one breast, one myeloma, 2 lymphoma, abnormal renal function tests (10), abnormal liver function tests (14);
- SACT not discontinued despite bilirubin levels greater than 100 µmol/L (4).

Case study 4

History

An elderly patient with locally advanced oesophageal cancer was only able to swallow liquids. On admission the patient was dehydrated, had obvious weight loss and a performance status of 3. Liver and renal function tests had been satisfactory three weeks earlier, but were not repeated prior to cycle 1 of cisplatin, epirubicin and capecitabine chemotherapy which was given at 100% doses.

Problems noted by the advisors

- SACT was inappropriate because of poor performance status
- Inappropriate timing of pre-treatment investigation.
- There had been no assessment of GFR prior to cisplatin chemotherapy
- Oral chemotherapy had been given in the presence of severe dysphagia.

Timing of investigations in relation to the first day of SACT

Essential pre-treatment investigations are undertaken within 72 hours of Day 1 of administration of each SACT cycle and also at various intervals throughout the cycle dependent on the SACT regimen used. The decision to give a cycle of SACT is made after the pre-treatment investigations have been reviewed.

Information from the data recorded on questionnaire A revealed that the time interval between the date of the decision to treat with the last cycle of SACT and Day 1 of administration was <72 hours in 61% (374/617) of patients, 4-7 days in 19% (117/617), 8-14 days in 10% (62/617), 15-21 days in 5% (32/617), 22-28 days in 2% (11/617) and >28 days in 3% (21/617) of cases (Figure 5.5).

In addition the time interval between the estimation of the full blood count and Day 1 of the last cycle of SACT was calculated using information from the data recorded on questionnaire A and the casenotes (Figure 5.6). This revealed that the time interval was <72 hours in 68% of case 259/379, 4-7 days in 12% (47/379), 8-14 days in 8% (30/379), 15-21 days in 4% (16/379), 22-28 days in 3% (10/379) and >28 days in 4% (17/379) of cases. The absence of a recent full blood count or other essential pre-treatment investigations was highlighted by the advisors as a cause for concern.

Pre-treatment assessment of previous toxicity and tumour response

---

STANDARDS

Toxicity should be clearly recorded for each cycle of chemotherapy using the Common Toxicity (CT) criteria. The outcomes of treatment should be monitored closely as treatment proceeds. Appropriate action should be taken if the side-effects are excessive and cannot be ameliorated, or if the cancer progresses.

Chemotherapy Guidelines: COIN 2001 Grade C[2]

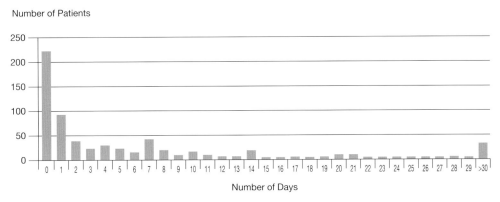

Figure 5.5 Time from decision to treat to SACT administration

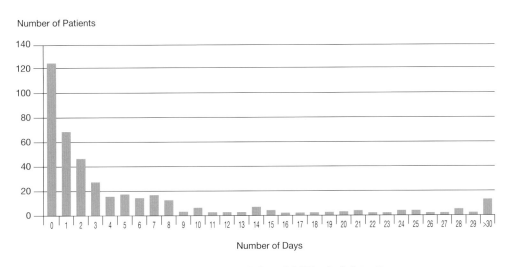

Figure 5.6 Time from FBC to SACT administration

Data from questionnaire A on the treatment cycle number were available in 582 cases. Table 5.6 shows that 52% (304/582) patients died following their first cycle of therapy. A further 48% (278/582) of cases had received one or more previous cycles of therapy.

Table 5.6 Number of cycles received

Cycle	Number of patients (%)
1	304 (52)
>1	278 (48)
Subtotal	**582**
Not answered	75
Total	**657**

The pre-treatment clinical assessments for patients receiving second or subsequent cycles of chemotherapy were reviewed by the advisors. Casenotes were provided in 267/278 cases. In general it was found that the recording of toxicity data and response data after each cycle of chemotherapy was poor.

Table 5.7 Pre-treatment assessments of toxicity

Assessment of toxicity	Number of patients (%)
Yes	170 (64)
No	97 (36)
Subtotal	267
Not Applicable – 1st cycle	203
Unknown	76
Total	546

An assessment of toxicity following the previous cycle was recorded in only 64% (170/267) of cases (Table 5.7), a toxicity check list being used in 26 cases. In 36% (97/267) of cases toxicity had not been recorded and insufficient records were provided to comment on 76 cases.

Toxicity check lists can improve the process of care when used as part of a clinical care pathway, can aid record keeping and be used as a clinical audit tool.

Table 5.8 Assessment of response to therapy

Assessment of response to therapy	Number of patients (%)
Yes	150 (54)
No	126 (46)
Subtotal	276
Not Applicable – 1st cycle	212
Unknown	58
Total	546

An assessment of response to therapy had been recorded in 54% (150/276) of cases, no record was made in 46% (126/276) of cases and insufficient data were provided to comment on 58 cases (Table 5.8).

Many of these cases may not have reached an appropriate time in the course of treatment to undertake an assessment of response.

SACT PRESCRIPTIONS AND DISPENSING

The working practices of the pharmacy departments were assessed by analysis of the data submitted on the 295 completed organisational questionnaires and detailed review by the pharmacists on the advisory panel of the 546 clinical case records

Pharmacy work load

As seen in Figure 5.7 SACT was prepared on site in 127 hospitals, off site in 70 hospitals and a combination of both in 85 hospitals. Off site preparation of SACT may have been undertaken by another NHS trust or from an external commercial organisation. No information was available on the preparation of SACT in 12 hospitals.

No information submitted from
12 organisations

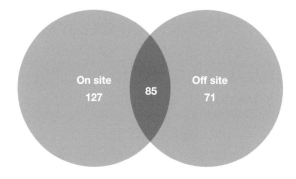

Figure 5.7 Preparation of SACT

Table 5.9 Numbers of doses of parenteral SACT dispensed per annum

Doses of SACT dispensed per annum							
Preparation	<2,000	2,000-9,999	10,000-20,000	>20,000	Subtotal	Unknown	Total
On site	24	60	20	12	**116**	11	127
Off site	38	12	1	1	**52**	19	71
Combination	18	34	15	8	**75**	10	85
Subtotal	80	106	36	21	243	40	283
Not answered	0	0	2	0	2	10	12
Total	80	106	38	21	245	50	295

Table 5.9 shows that the number of doses of parenteral SACT dispensed annually was <2000 in 33% (80/243), 2,000-9,999 in 44% (106/243), 10,000-20,000 in 16% (38/243) and >20.000 in 9% (21/243) of pharmacy departments.

It can be seen from Figure 5.8 that all cancer centres dispensed more than 2000 prescriptions of pSACT each year. The only hospitals dispensing more than 20,000 doses of pSACT per year were cancer centres and two district general hospitals. At the other end of the scale, most independent hospitals dispensed relatively few doses of pSACT, as did five NHS teaching hospitals and 12 district general hospitals.

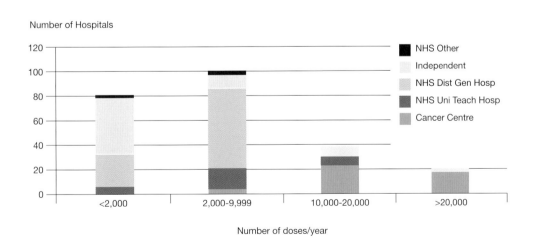

Figure 5.8 Categories of hospitals dispensing annual doses of parenteral SACT

Prescriptions

SACT prescriptions are complex. A cycle of treatment often consists of a number of different chemo-therapeutic agents administered on different days of the cycle, via different routes of administration and over different time periods. The regimen may include a period of pre and/or post treatment hydration and prophylactic anti-emetics. The prescriptions are therefore time consuming to write and a potential source of error. To reduce clinical risk some centres have replaced hand-written with pre-printed prescriptions or the use of electronic prescribing. A further advantage of an electronic system is the routine prospective data collation for clinical audit.

When prescribing parenteral SACT 155 organisations reported that they used a single prescription format: hand-written (42); pre-printed (97) and electronic (16). A further 115 organisations used a combination of two or all three formats. Twenty five organisations did not provide information (Figure 5.9).

The prescriptions for parenteral SACT were available for review by the pharmacist advisors in 305 cases. It can be seen from Table 5.10 that of these, 23% (70/305) were hand-written, 48% (147/305) pre-printed and 29% (88/305) in an electronic format. Data from the organisational question also showed that only 23/49 (one not answered) of the cancer centres actually had electronic prescribing.

STANDARD

All prescriptions of cytotoxic chemotherapy agents should be computer-generated at least when using regimens from the agreed list.

Manual for Cancer Services: Department of Health 2004 3C-210[1]

Table 5.10 Format of prescriptions for parenteral SACT

Format	Number of patients (%)
Hand-written prescription	70 (23)
Pre-printed prescription	147 (48)
Electronic prescription	88 (29)
Total	305

Parenteral SACT

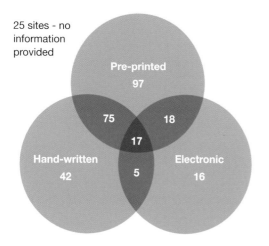

25 sites - no information provided

Figure 5.9 Type of prescription used for parenteral SACT

Oral SACT

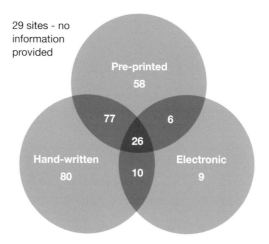

29 sites - no information provided

Figure 5.10 Type of prescription used for oral SACT

When prescribing oral SACT, 147 organisations reported that they used a single prescription format: hand-written (80), pre-printed (58), electronic (9), whilst 119 organisations used a combination of different formats. A further 29 organisations did not provide information (Figure 5.10).

Table 5.11 Format of prescriptions for oral SACT

Format	Number of patients (%)
Hand-written prescription	53 (44)
Pre-printed prescription	46 (38)
Electronic prescription	22 (18)
Total	**121**

Table 5.11 shows that 121 prescriptions for oral SACT were available for review by the pharmacist advisors. Of these 44% (53/121) were hand-written, 38% (46/121) pre-printed and 18% (22/121) in an electronic format.

Prescriptions assessed by pharmacist advisors
The study showed that parenteral chemotherapy was most commonly prescribed on pre-printed prescriptions, whilst oral chemotherapy was prescribed on hand-written scripts (Figure 5.11).

Percent of cases

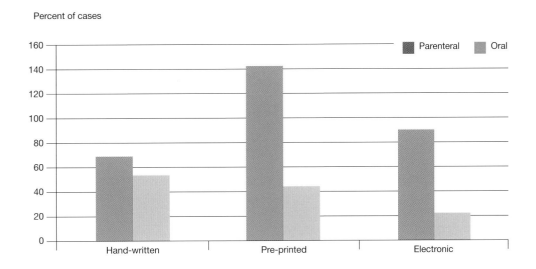

Figure 5.11 Format of SACT prescriptions

The advisors noted that in many instances the hand-written prescriptions for parenteral chemotherapy were of poor quality, with additions and crossings out. It was the advisors' opinion that this posed a considerable risk for error.

Commercially available electronic prescribing systems are designed to produce prescriptions for parenteral chemotherapy. In the advisors' view the prescriptions for oral chemotherapy were often over designed and confusing and at present are a potential source for error. This may be the reason many centres still use hand-written or locally produced pre-printed prescriptions for oral chemotherapy.

Pre-dispensing safety checks

In order to reduce clinical risk various systems have been established to check the accuracy of chemotherapy prescriptions before the drugs are dispensed.

STANDARD

All cytotoxic chemotherapy prescriptions should be checked and authorised by a pharmacist.
Manual for Cancer Services: Department of Health 2004 3C-209[1]

Table 5.12 Prescription checked by a pharmacist

Prescription		
Checked by pharmacist	Parenteral (%)	Oral (%)
Yes	265 (97)	194 (73)
No	9 (3)	71 (27)
Subtotal	274	265
Unknown	5	9
Not answered	16	21
Total	295	295

Table 5.13 Safety checks performed

Pharmacist safety checks		
Performed	Dose calculations (%)	Investigation results (%)
Yes	261 (96)	192 (70)
No	10 (4)	81 (30)
Subtotal	271	273
Unknown	9	5
Not answered	15	17
Total	295	295

The study showed that pharmacists with specific oncology knowledge and experience checked all parenteral SACT scripts in 265 hospitals and all oral SACT scripts in 194 hospitals (Table 5.12). The safety checks included checking the dose calculation (261 hospitals) and checking the essential pre-treatment investigation results (192 hospitals) (Table 5.13). The advisors noted that oral SACT prescriptions were not checked by a cancer pharmacist in 71 organisations. Oral therapies can be associated with as much clinical risk as parenteral treatments and therefore safety check should be in place.

Review by the advisors of the 369 available prescriptions showed there was evidence that the prescription had been checked by a pharmacist in only 53% (196/369) of cases. This falls well below the accepted standard.

The hospital pharmacist had identified three inaccuracies which had lead to an adjustment in the dose of SACT prescribed. In one case the patient had lost weight and the drug doses had not been recalculated, in the second case the level of creatinine was unacceptable for full drug dosage and in the third case the dose of carboplatin had been based on serum creatinine and not on creatinine clearance.

Case study 5

History

A patient was prescribed a first cycle of SACT. A dose error was identified by the pharmacist but the clinicians appeared not to have received the information or not to have acted on it. An inappropriately high dose of SACT was administered and the patient developed overwhelming complications. Neutropenia was not managed well and the patient died of sepsis.

Problems noted by the advisors

- An example of how errors can cascade and contribute to a patient's death
- An error in calculation
- Poor communication between team members involved in the prescribing and dispensing of SACT
- Subsequent treatment of neutropenia was sub-optimal.

Case study 6

History

A middle aged patient with a significant cardiac history was being treated with palliative intent for recurrent upper gastrointestinal cancer. It was intended that the patient would have had a cardiac work up prior to SACT but due to a misunderstanding between clinicians this never happened. Each clinician thought the other had ordered the cardiac investigations. The patient received drugs inappropriate for someone with cardiac problems and died of a myocardial infarction.

Problems noted by the advisors

- Poor communication between team members
- Patient received inappropriate drugs
- The risk of cardiac events was recorded on the consent form. This should have acted as a reminder to review the cardiac investigation.

The pharmacist advisors identified 10 cases where the drug doses had been incorrectly calculated and 12 cases where there was a potential drug interaction e.g. fluconazole and vincristine, capecitabine and warfarin, diclofenac and gabapentin. One pre-printed prescription was identified where the recommended dose of cisplatin was too high – fortunately the prescriber did not use the recommendation.

Pharmacists' training in SACT dispensing

Pharmacists, who undertook the SACT prescription safety checks, underwent specialist training in 50 organisations and followed written protocols in 43 hospitals. No information was available from 210 organisations. However, 21 hospitals reported that the pharmacists did not have any specialist training and 24 hospitals did not have protocols for the pharmacists to follow.

ADMINISTRATION OF SACT

Place of administration of SACT

When possible SACT is administered in an out-patient setting – this is both cost effective and more acceptable to the patient and their family than a hospital admission. Some hospitals have introduced a domiciliary service where selected intravenous regimens can be administered at the patient's home.

Analysis of the data recorded on questionnaire A revealed that 35% (221/636) of patients who died within 30 days of SACT received their treatment as an in-patient, 57% (364/636) as an out patient and 8% (51/636) in their own home. No information was available in 21 cases.

The patients who received their SACT at home were all taking oral or subcutaneous medication (capecitabine, vinorelbine, etoposide, interferon, chlorambucil, hydroxycarbamide, cytarabine). A "chemotherapy at home" service administering intravenous SACT was not used for any of the patients within this study.

The number of patients receiving in-patient therapy was relatively high. This was likely to be a reflection of the relative poor performance status and the advanced disease of the patients included in this study.

Designated area of the hospital

SACT should be administered within a designated area of the hospital where there are facilities for dealing with any immediate complication as defined in the standards below.

STANDARDS

Cytotoxic chemotherapy should be carried out in designated facilities which are properly equipped for the purpose.

Good Practice Guidance for Clinical Oncologists: Royal College of Radiologists 2003[18]

There should be a written policy whereby inpatient chemotherapy (where patients stay overnight) should only be given on named wards where it is agreed as part of the ward's regular activity and to which such patients are admitted in preference to other wards.

Manual for Cancer Services: Department of Health 2004 3C-104[1]

In-patient treatments were administered on oncology wards (87 cases), haemato-oncology wards (69 cases), chemotherapy wards (51 cases), general medical wards (8 cases), intensive care units (4 cases), a gynaecology ward (1 case) and the urology department (1 case receiving intravesical chemotherapy).

Out-patient treatments were administered in designated chemotherapy units (243 cases), day care units (55 cases) or out patient clinics (66 cases).

Route of administration of SACT

Systemic anti-cancer therapies are most commonly administered intravenously as a bolus or short infusion. The increasing use of continuous low dose rate infusions and the development of more oral chemotherapeutic agents have enabled patients to receive treatment in their own homes.

Table 5.14 Route of administration of SACT

	Number of patients (%)
IV peripheral	122 (32)
IV through central line	61 (16)
IV unspecified	81 (21)
Oral	83 (22)
Oral/IV peripheral	18 (5)
Subcutaneous	9 (2)
Other	9 (2)
Subtotal	**383**
Unknown	163
Total	**546**

The advisors reviewed 546 case records. The route of administration of SACT could be determined in 383 cases. Of these cases 22% (83/383) of treatment was oral, 32% (122/383) intravenous via a peripheral line, 16% (61/383) intravenous via a central line and 21% (81/383) intravenous line not specified. Other modes of administration used were subcutaneous (9) or intrathecal (1). A combination of different modalities was recorded in 22 patients. In 163 the route could not be identified from the casenotes.

Central venous lines

Central venous lines are used for the administration of some SACT regimens in order to reduce the incidence of peripheral thrombophlebitis, to enable continuous low rate intravenous infusions to be administered in the patient's home and to increase the quality of life in those patients requiring multiple treatments and support with transfusions of red cells and platelets.

STANDARDS

The facility should have at least one named clinical specialist in the insertion of semi-permanent aids to venous access (eg for illustration - central venous or Portacath lines). They should have time designated in their list of duties or timetable for the insertion of such aids when required.

Note: They may be medically qualified or a nurse.

Manual for Cancer Services: Department of Health 2004 3C-418[1]

Two-dimensional (2-D) imaging ultrasound guidance is recommended as the preferred method for insertion of central venous catheters (CVCs) into the internal jugular vein (IJV) in adults and children in elective situations.

Guidance on the use of ultrasound locating devices for placing central venous catheters, Technology Appraisal No. 49: NICE 2002[6]

Indwelling venous catheters are used to deliver intensive chemotherapy. These should only be handled by designated staff members, since scrupulous hygiene and expertise are essential. Insertion should be carried out in dedicated areas (special procedure room or operating room) and real-time imaging should be available. Trainees must be closely supervised by personnel with documented competence in such supervision. Central venous or Portacath catheter insertion must be available by a committed and experienced specialist.

Improving outcomes in haematological cancers: NICE 2003[7]

Type of line used

The study revealed that Hickman or Groshong lines were used in 260/289 hospitals, peripherally inserted central lines (PICC lines) in 220/289 and portacaths, implantable ports, in 144/289 hospitals. No information was received from six hospitals.

Central venous line placement

Central venous lines were placed in theatre (168), X-ray departments (146) or in a Day unit (206). Other areas of the hospital used included wards (53), treatment rooms (39) or the intensive care unit (2).

Staff involved in the work of placing and removing central venous lines

From Figure 5.13 it can be seen that the lines were placed by radiologists (141), specialist nurses (116), surgeons (103), and anaesthetists (99). Other members of staff who undertook this work were medical members of the oncology/haemato-oncology teams (34), general physicians (6), intravenous access teams (6) and specialist radiographers (4).

The lines were removed mainly by medical members of the oncology/haemato-oncology teams (158) or specialist nurses (146). Other members of staff involved in this work included surgeons (83), radiologists (38) and anaesthetists (37).

Percent of hospitals

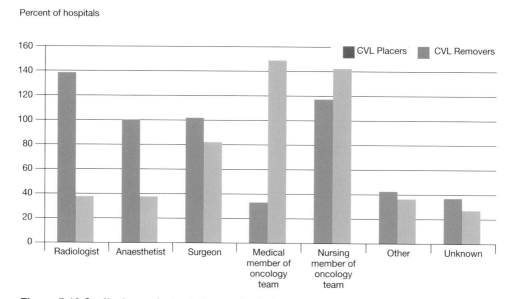

Figure 5.13 Staff who undertook the work of placing and removing central venous lines

NICE guidance

The National Institute of Health and Clinical Excellence (NICE) technology appraisal 49 – guidance on 2D ultrasound guided placement of central venous lines was published in 2002[7]. Information from the organisational questionnaires suggested that at the time of the enquiry (2006), this guidance had been implemented in 88% (207/236) of organisations that answered this question. The 29 organisations that had not implemented the guidance were seven independent hospitals, 13 district general hospitals and four teaching hospitals and five cancer centres.

Anticoagulation

One of the complications associated with the use of central venous lines is line thromboses. Only a small percentage of organisations routinely anticoagulate patients who have central venous lines inserted - 15% (39/260) of organisations that use Hickman or Groshong lines, 11% (25/225) that use PICC lines and 11% (16/145) that use Portacaths. When anticoagulation was used, 47 centres used low dose warfarin at 1 mg/day, nine centres aimed to achieve an INR of 1.5-2.0 and eight centres aimed to achieve an INR of 2-3.

One hundred and thirty five organisations had a local protocol for the management of central line thrombosis, 104 centres did not and information was not available from 56 hospitals.

Training of specialist chemotherapy nurses

STANDARDS
Chemotherapy must be administered only by staff considered to be appropriately trained according to local clinical governance requirements in all settings in which they work.
Good Practice for Clinical Oncologists: Royal College of Radiologists 2003[18]

For clinical chemotherapy services which are being visited for peer review two or more years after publication of the chemotherapy measures, each staff member on the list of those competent to administer chemotherapy should have written confirmation that their competence has been re-assessed and reconfirmed annually.
Manual for Cancer Services: Department of Health 2004 3C 151[1]

Chemotherapy specific training was provided before nurses are authorised to administer SACT in 263 organisations. Nine organisations reported that they did not provide training (six independent, one NHS district general hospital, one NHS teaching hospital and one NHS other) and no information was received from 23 hospitals.

Safety checks pre-administration

STANDARD
Doctors or specialist nurses who administer chemotherapy must perform checks with a colleague to confirm patient identity, drug regimen, dosage, route of administration and frequency. If there is any doubt treatment must not proceed.
Good Practice for Clinical Oncologists: Royal College of Radiologists 2003[18]

The organisational data demonstrated that a policy was in place for SACT to be checked by a second nurse, prior to administration in 89% (256/289) of organisations. However, 33 hospitals did not have a policy and no information was available from six hospitals.

Review by clinical advisors revealed that there was evidence in the clinical case record that SACT had been checked by two nurses, prior to administration, in only 71% (146/207) of cases. It was not checked in 61 cases and was not documented to review 339 cases.

Complications related to SACT administration
The administration of SACT can be associated with a number of acute side effects. In order to minimise risk, each organisation should have protocols in place to ensure safe delivery of chemotherapy and rapid assessment and treatment of the most common complications.

STANDARDS
The areas/wards/rooms identified for SACT administration should have available in them:
- The regimen details as per the network list of acceptable regimens, for the regimens in use.
- Protocol documents and equipment for the management of at least the following emergencies:
  i. Anaphylactic shock
  ii. Extravasation of cytotoxics
  iii. Cardiac arrest
  iv. Spillage of cytotoxics
Manual for Cancer Services: Department of Health 2004 3C-106[1]

There should be guidelines/protocols covering the following:
- Cytotoxic administration techniques.
- The recognition and treatment of cytotoxic extravasation.
- The recognition and treatment of allergic reactions including anaphylaxis.
Manual for Cancer Services: Department of Health 2004 3C-116, 123 & 124[1]

From the 295 organisational questionnaires five
protocols were available (Table 5.15):

Table 5.15 Protocols available

	Yes (%)	No (%)	Subtotal	Not answered	Total
Administration of intrathecal chemotherapy	210 (80)	54 (20)	**264**	31	**295**
Chemotherapy extravasation	277 (97)	8 (3)	**285**	10	**295**
Chemotherapy anaphylaxis	270 (95)	14 (5)	**284**	11	**295**
Management of central line thrombosis	135 (56)	104 (44)	**239**	56	**295**
Anticoagulation policy	221 (85)	40 (15)	**261**	34	**295**

The presence of a policy for the administration of
intrathecal chemotherapy was part of the last peer review
process[28]. NCEPOD noted that 54 hospitals did not have
a policy for intrathecal chemotherapy administration (Table
5.15). The 54 organisations included 38 independent
hospitals, 13 district general hospitals, one teaching
hospital and one cancer centre. Intrathecal chemotherapy
may not be administered at these sites but this information
was not available from this study.

***Complications during or immediately following SACT
administration***

Sufficient documentation was available for the advisors
to comment on 435/546 cases reviewed. Only 14/435
patients were reported as suffering an immediate
complication associated with the administration of SACT.
These included chest pain in a patient receiving rituximab,
an irinotecan acute cholinergic reaction, vomiting and
cellulitis of left arm.

Key findings

Three hospitals permitted SHO/ST1/2 doctors to initiate a course of SACT.

19 hospitals permitted SHO/ST1/2 doctors to prescribe a second or subsequent cycle of SACT.

Four hospitals allowed junior doctors to prescribe cycles of SACT from the moment of employment, with no assessment of competency or training programme.

52% (304/582) of patients in this study who died within 30 days of receiving SACT, died following cycle 1 of a course of SACT.

Essential pre-treatment investigations were omitted in 14% (64/461) of patients.

There was failure to act upon unacceptable pre-treatment investigations in 65/77 cases.

There was no record of the presence or absence of toxicity following the previous cycle of SACT in 36% (97/267) of cases.

No assessment of tumour response was made in 46% (126/276) of patients.

In only 53% (196/369) of cases was there evidence that a pharmacist had checked the SACT prescription.

In only 71% (146/201) of cases was there evidence that SACT had been checked by two nurses prior to administration.

Recommendations

Junior medical staff at FY1, FY2, ST1 and ST2 grade should not be authorised to initiate SACT. *(Clinical directors)*

All independent and supplementary prescribers (specialist chemotherapy nurses and cancer pharmacists) and junior medical staff should be locally trained/accredited, following attendance at a supplementary prescribers' course, before being authorised to prescribe SACT. *(Cancer services managers and clinical directors)*

The results of a pre-treatment full blood count and renal and liver functions tests should be assessed before each cycle of chemotherapy. *(Clinical directors)*

Toxicity check lists should be developed to assist record keeping and aid the process of care in prescribing SACT. *(Cancer services managers and clinical directors)*

Assessment of tumour response to treatment should be undertaken and recorded at appropriate intervals depending on the treatment intent and SACT regimen used. *(Consultant oncologists and clinical directors)*

All SACT prescriptions should be checked by a pharmacist who has undergone specialist training, demonstrated their competence and are locally authorised/accredited for the task. This applies to oral as well as parenteral treatments. *(Clinical directors and pharmacists)*

Pharmacists should sign the SACT prescription to indicate that it has been verified and validated for the intended patient and that all the safety checks have been undertaken. *(Pharmacists)*

6 – Safety of SACT

Introduction

As with all medical intervention, the possible risks of systemic anti-cancer therapy (SACT) must be considered against the potential benefits. The dose of SACT required to be effective in controlling tumour growth must be considered against a dose which produces clinically significant toxicity.

The dose and timing of each cycle of chemotherapy is adjusted depending on the patient's clinical condition, previous toxicity and pre-treatment investigations. However, some patients will still suffer severe side effects. The care of these patients can be optimised by providing clear patient information regarding emergency assessments, having good communication and rapid referral pathways between different health professionals, ensuring rapid assessment of the ill patient and appropriate and timely management of oncological emergencies. Regular prospective clinical audit of toxicity and review of all treatment related deaths within clinical governance programmes would contribute to the continuous improvement of the service provided.

Patient information on seeking emergency advice and review

STANDARD
There should be a system which ensures that patients receive appropriate advice and care at any time, day or night, should they suffer unexpected consequences of treatment.
Good Practice Guide for Clinical Oncologists: Royal College of Radiologists 2003[18]

STANDARD
There should be written information for patients and carers covering the action they should take, whom they should contact for advice, and the symptoms that should prompt this, with regards to the following complications of chemotherapy:
- Neutropenic sepsis.
- Cytotoxic extravasation.
- Nausea and vomiting.
- Stomatitis, other mucositis and diarrhoea.
Manual for Cancer Services: Department of Health 2004 3C-132[1]

Patients who become unwell following SACT must get appropriate advice and be seen quickly in order to minimise treatment related morbidity and mortality.

Patient information on the side effects of treatment should be provided by the oncologist within outpatient clinics and specialist nurses or pharmacists in patient education clinics. The verbal information should be supplemented by patient information leaflets and telephone follow up after administration of treatment. Patients should be advised to contact the chemotherapy telephone helpline if they become unwell. The helpline should be manned by specialist chemotherapy nurses who give advice or arrange an assessment by a member of the medical staff as appropriate. Patients should be provided with chemotherapy ID cards in order to alert health professionals to the fact that the patient has recently received chemotherapy and includes contact details of the cancer team providing care.

Patients should be given clear written instructions about when and how to obtain advice if they become severely unwell.

It is clear from Tables 6.1 and 6.2 that almost all NHS and independent hospitals claim to provide written guidance on when and how to seek advice in the event of becoming unwell.

Table 6.1 Written guidance for patients with solid tumours

	Written guidance on when and how to seek advice				
	Yes	No	Subtotal	Not answered	Total
Cancer Centre	50	0	50	0	50
NHSUniTeachHosp	21	0	21	12	33
NHSDistGenHosp	105	3	108	17	125
Independent	68	4	72	6	78
NHSOther	3	2	5	4	9
Total	247	9	256	39	295

Table 6.2 Written guidance for patients with haematological malignancies

	Written guidance on when and how to seek advice				
	Yes	No	Subtotal	Not answered	Total
Cancer Centre	44	0	44	6	50
NHSUniTeachHosp	29	0	29	4	33
NHSDistGenHosp	116	3	119	6	125
Independent	44	6	50	28	78
NHSOther	4	2	6	3	9
Total	237	11	248	47	295

Patient information on emergency advice and review

Table 6.3 How patients could have obtained further help

	Yes (%)	No (%)	Subtotal	Not answered	Total
Dedicated phone line	187 (66)	97 (34)	284	11	295
Nurse led patient education clinics	121 (44)	155 (56)	276	19	295
Pharmacist led patient education clinics	10 (4)	260 (96)	270	25	295
SACT info card	264 (95)	13 (5)	277	18	295
Follow up phone call	72 (27)	196 (73)	268	27	295

Table 6.3 details other ways in which patients might receive information on what do do if they become unwell after receiving SACT. In addition to written information, nurse led education clinics may be helpful in meeting the needs of patients for information. They are likely to be of most use for patients with the more common cancers and

in some hospitals are found useful for patients receiving oral SACT. Such clinics were found in about half of the NHS hospitals delivering SACT but are less common in Independent hospitals (Table 6.4). In 10 hospitals such clinics were led by specialist pharmacists.

Table 6.4 Nurse led patient education clinics

	Yes	No	Subtotal	Not answered	Total
Cancer Centre	29	20	49	1	50
NHSUniTeachHosp	13	17	30	3	33
NHSDistGenHosp	59	60	119	6	125
Independent	19	54	73	5	78
NHSOther	1	4	5	4	9
Total	121	155	276	19	295

Some hospitals have also introduced a policy of telephoning patients soon after they have started SACT to ensure that they have not encountered any unexpectedly severe side effects. This approach appeared to be more common in independent hospitals than NHS hospitals, where the district general hospitals are more likely to follow up with a telephone call than the teaching hospitals and cancer centres (Table 6.5).

Table 6.5 Follow up phone calls

	Yes	No	Subtotal	Not answered	Total
Cancer Centre	8	40	48	2	50
NHSUniTeachHosp	3	27	30	3	33
NHSDistGenHosp	38	86	124	1	125
Independent	30	39	69	9	78
NHSOther	1	4	5	4	9
Total	80	196	276	19	295

Nearly one in three hospitals from which information was received did not have a (24 hour) dedicated phone line for patients to ring if they needed advice (Table 6.6).

Table 6.6 Dedicated phone line

	Dedicated phone line				
	Yes	No	Subtotal	Not answered	Total
Cancer Centre	38	12	50	0	50
NHSUniTeachHosp	21	11	32	1	33
NHSDistGenHosp	82	39	121	4	12
Independent	42	34	76	2	78
NHSOther	4	1	5	4	9
Total	187	97	284	11	295

Emergency admissions policies

As well as providing written information to the patient about how to seek advice most NHS hospitals had written policies for the emergency admission of patients who become unwell after SACT. Such policies were less common in the independent hospitals (Tables 6.7 and 6.8). All hospitals delivering SACT should maintain up to date emergency admission policies for patients who subsequently become unwell. If they do not admit patients with complications of SACT the policy should detail what steps should be taken to ensure that any patient contacting the hospital for advice will be admitted to an appropriate hospital if needed.

Table 6.7 Emergency admissions policy for patients with solid tumours

	Emergency admissions policy for patients receiving SACT				
	Yes	No	Subtotal	Not answered	Total
Cancer Centre	45	5	50	0	50
NHSUniTeachHosp	16	5	21	12	33
NHSDistGenHosp	89	16	105	20	125
Independent	46	30	76	2	78
NHSOther	2	4	6	3	9
Total	198	60	258	37	295

Table 6.8 Emergency admissions policy for patients with haematological malignancies

	Emergency admissions policy for patients receiving SACT				
	Yes	**No**	**Subtotal**	**Not answered**	**Total**
Cancer Centre	40	3	**43**	7	50
NHSUniTeachHosp	24	5	**29**	4	33
NHSDistGenHosp	100	15	**115**	10	125
Independent	30	21	**51**	27	78
NHSOther	4	2	**6**	3	9
Total	**198**	**46**	**244**	**51**	**295**

Grade 3 and 4 toxicity

STANDARD

For 100% of patients, treatment of toxicity should be clearly recorded for each cycle of chemotherapy using the Common Toxicity Criteria.

Chemotherapy Guidelines: COIN 2001[2]

Incidence of toxicity

Information on treatment related toxicity following the last cycle of SACT was collected by local clinicians completing questionnaire B (659 cases) and the detailed review of the clinical case records by the advisory panel (546 cases). The data were recorded using the Common Toxicity Criteria (See Appendix 5).

Doctors were asked to record grade 3 and grade 4 events and toxicities. A grade 3 or 4 event is not necessarily related to the treatment given. A grade 3 or 4 toxicity is treatment related.

The local clinician, caring for the patient at the time of death, was asked whether the patient suffered any grade 3 or 4 toxicity related to the most recent cycle of SACT. The question was not answered on 145/659 of questionnaires B. Of the remaining 514 cases, 43% (220/514) of patients were considered to have suffered grade 3 or 4 toxicity (Table 6.9).

Table 6.9 Grade 3/4 toxicity in the view of the clinician completing the questionnaire.

Grade 3/4 toxicity	Number of patients (%)
Yes	220 (43)
No	294 (57)
Subtotal	**514**
Unknown	86
Not answered	59
Total	**659**

In addition the advisory panel were asked whether the patient had suffered a grade 3 or 4 event following their most recent cycle of SACT. From Table 6.10 it can be seen that there was insufficient documentation to comment on 102 of the cases reviewed. From the remaining 444 sets of casenotes 250 patients suffered a grade 3/4 event. The findings by the advisors were compared to the answers given by the local clinician completing questionnaire B (Table 6.11)

Table 6.10 Advisors' view of whether the patient had suffered a grade 3 or 4 event

Grade 3/4 event	Number of patients (%)
Yes	250 (56)
No	194 (44)
Subtotal	**444**
Unknown	102
Total	**546**

Table 6.11 Grade 3/4 toxicity recorded on questionnaire B (QB) and the advisors' assessment form (AF)

Grade 3/4 toxicity	QB cases	% of patients with toxicity	AF cases	% of patients with toxicity
Neutropenia	134	26	124	28
Neutropenic sepsis	83	16	104	23
Infection	111	22	116	26
Thrombocytopaenia	80	16	79	18
Haemorrhage	15	3	22	5
Thrombosis	10	2	13	3
Stomatitis	14	3	21	5
Vomiting	42	8	54	12
Diarrhoea	41	8	54	12
Renal impairment	61	12	72	16
Liver impairment	27	5	30	7
Hypomagnesaemia	21	4	4	<1
Hypokalaemia	15	3	15	3
Hypercalcaemia	4	<1	1	<1
Myocardial ischaemia	11	2	12	3
Arrhythmia	14	3	10	2
Multi-organ failure	21	4	25	6
Tumour lysis syndrome	1	<1	2	<1
Anaphylaxis	2	<1	0	<1
Total number of G3/4 toxicity	**707**		**758**	
Total number of patients	**514**		**444**	

Relationship of the grade 3/4 event to SACT given

The advisors were asked to assess whether the grade 3 and grade 4 events occurred as a direct consequence of the treatment given (Table 6.12). In their opinion the events were directly related to treatment in 54% (440/820), probably related 21% (174/820) and possibly related in 18% (144/820) of episodes. In only 8% (62/820) of events was it thought that it was not related to therapy. There were insufficient data to comment in 123 events.

Table 6.12 Advisors' view of whether the grade 3/4 event was related to the SACT

Grade 3/4 event	Definitely	Probably	Possibly	Not related	Insufficient data	Total G3/4 event
Neutropenia	107	13	4	2	3	129
Neutropenic sepsis	82	14	8	1	4	109
Infection	49	33	34	9	10	135
Thrombocytopaenia	68	4	7	4	3	86
Haemorrhage	10	6	6	6	4	32
Thrombosis	3	2	8	3	4	20
Stomatitis	12	8	1	-	13	34
Vomiting	22	21	11	1	7	62
Diarrhoea	25	22	7	3	9	66
Renal impairment	28	21	23	11	4	87
Liver impairment	8	10	12	9	4	43
Hypomagnesaemia	2	1	1	1	16	21
Hypokalaemia	5	3	7	1	4	20
Hypercalcaemia	-	1	-	3	7	11
Myocardial ischaemia	2	4	6	-	5	17
Arrhythmia	3	5	2	1	10	21
Multi-organ failure	13	6	6	6	5	36
Tumour lysis syndrome	1	-	1	1	6	9
Anaphylaxis	-	-	-	-	5	5
Total	**440**	**174**	**144**	**62**	**123**	**943**

Effect of the toxicity

The clinical effect of high grade toxicity varies depending on the organ involved and the medical condition of the patient. Treatment related toxicity is expected and acceptable when treating patients with potentially curative SACT such as the treatment of acute leukaemia. However 93% (441/476) of the patients in this study, with solid tumours received palliative therapy. The aim of such treatment is to alleviate symptoms of disease with the minimum amount of treatment side effects. 73% (170/233) of patients receiving palliative treatment suffered G3/4 toxicity, in 17 cases the treatment intent was unknown as there was no questionnaire A returned. This level of toxicity may have been related to the patients' poor performance status, co-morbidities, multiple previous treatments and an inappropriate decision to treat with the last course or cycle of SACT. It may also have been due to inappropriate timing and/or dosing of the last SACT cycle. These factors were analysed further.

Table 6.13 Type of assessment for patients with a grade 3/4 event

Type of assessment for patients with a grade 3/4 event	%
Attended emergency department	40 (18)
Urgent hospital admission	55 (25)
Urgent hospital review/appointment	21 (9)
Current inpatient assessment	45 (20)
GP review	18 (8)
Routine hospital appointment	16 (7)
Chemotherapy helpline	6 (3)
Phone conversation	8 (4)
Other	13 (6)
Subtotal	222
Not documented	28
Total	250

Dose and time scheduling of SACT

Analysis of the data from the local oncologist (questionnaire A) revealed that 79% (494/624) of patients received full doses of SACT at the scheduled treatment time, 14% (86/624) had a dose reduction, 6% (36/624) had a treatment delay, and in 1% (8/624) of cases the SACT was both delayed and dose reduced. No information was available in 33 cases (Table 6.14).

Table 6.14 Adjustment to treatment received by patients

Treatment	Number of patients (%)
Given as planned	494 (79)
Dose reduction	86 (14)
Delayed	36 (6)
Delayed/dose reduction	8 (1)
Subtotal	624
Unknown	33
Total	657

The reason for treatment delays included neutropenia, palliative radiotherapy, chest infection, general deterioration and reason for dose reductions included poor performance status, impaired liver function and previous neutropenia.

Advisors' opinion on dose and timing of SACT

The advisors were asked to review the last SACT prescription in order to assess whether appropriate doses of drugs had been used and whether the treatment had been given at an appropriate time.

Table 6.15 shows that the SACT regimen had been reduced and/or delayed in 32% (151/479) of cases. This is a greater percentage than that quoted by the local oncologist (21%; 130/624) and may reflect more detailed review of the casenotes by the advisory panel. In the 546 cases reviewed there was insufficient documentation to comment on 67 cases.

Table 6.15 Adjustments to treatment recommended by the advisors

Treatment	Number of patients (%)
Given as planned	328 (68)
Dose reduction	85 (18)
Delayed	39 (8)
Delayed/dose reduction	27 (6)
Subtotal	**479**
Insufficient data	67
Total	**546**

Dose reductions

The dose of chemotherapy had been reduced in 23% of cases (112/479) for the following reasons: poor performance status, age, impaired liver function, impaired renal function, or previous haematological toxicity.

The treatment was given at full doses in 77% (367/479) of cases. In the opinion of the advisors the chemotherapy doses should have been reduced in 13% (46/367) (see Figure 6.17) of cases for the following reasons: impaired renal or liver function, poor performance status, previous haematological toxicity, heavily pre-treated patient.

Case study 7

History

A middle aged patient with small cell lung cancer and mediastinal lymphadenopathy was admitted with diarrhoea 5 days following the third cycle of SACT. The chemotherapy had been given at 100% doses. This cycle of treatment had been delayed one week because of a neutropenia (neut 0.6) following cycle 2. On examination the patient was dehydrated, dyspnoeic and neutropenic (neut=0.1). Faecal culture revealed clostridium difficile infection and blood cultures revealed an enterococcal septicaemia. The patient was treated with IV antibiotics and GCSF.

Problems noted by the advisors
- No SACT dose reduction despite toxicity following previous cycle of SACT.

Treatment delays

SACT was delayed in 14% of cases (66/479) for the following reasons: haematological toxicity, infection, administration reasons, implementation of another treatment e.g. radiotherapy, paracentesis.

The treatment was given at the scheduled time in 86% (413/479) of cases. In the opinion of the advisors the treatment should have been delayed in 14% (58/413) of cases for the following reasons: poor renal or liver function, haematological toxicity, poor performance status, result of EDTA clearance not available.

Case study 8

History

A patient with lung cancer had a 6 week delay between discussion at an MDT meeting and actually meeting a medical oncologist at a peripheral clinic. There was a further 2 week delay starting treatment. The SACT given differed from that recommended by the MDT. The patient died 8 days after starting SACT.

Problems noted by the advisors

- Did the long delay contribute to this patient's death?
- The delay in starting SACT seemed to be entirely administrative
- The SACT given was different to that agreed with no explanation for the change of plan.

Overall opinion on the decision to give the last cycle of SACT

The overall opinion of the advisors was that the decision to give the last cycle of SACT at the dose and schedule given was appropriate in 65% (281/435). However, they judged that it was inappropriate in 35% (154/435). No opinion was given on 111 cases (Table 6.16).

Table 6.16 Advisors' view of the appropriateness of the SACT administration

Appropriate to give cycle at the doses given	Number of patients (%)
Yes	281 (65)
No	154 (35)
Subtotal	435
Unknown	111
Total	546

The reasons the last cycle of SACT was considered inappropriate can be seen in Table 6.17.

Table 6.17 Reasons why the SACT was judged inappropriate in the view of the advisors (answers may be multiple)

Reason	Number of patients
Essential pre-treatment investigations not undertaken	14
Abnormal haematology/biochemistry	52
Progressive disease	51
Dose reduction required in view of previous toxicity	19
Patient still suffering toxicity from previous cycle	8
Co-morbidity	24
Other reasons	57
Number of patients reviewed	435
Inappropriate dose or timing of SACT	154
225 reasons in 154 patients	

It is important to note that 12% (51/435) of patients had chemotherapy when in the advisors' opinion it was inappropriate as they had obvious progression of disease.

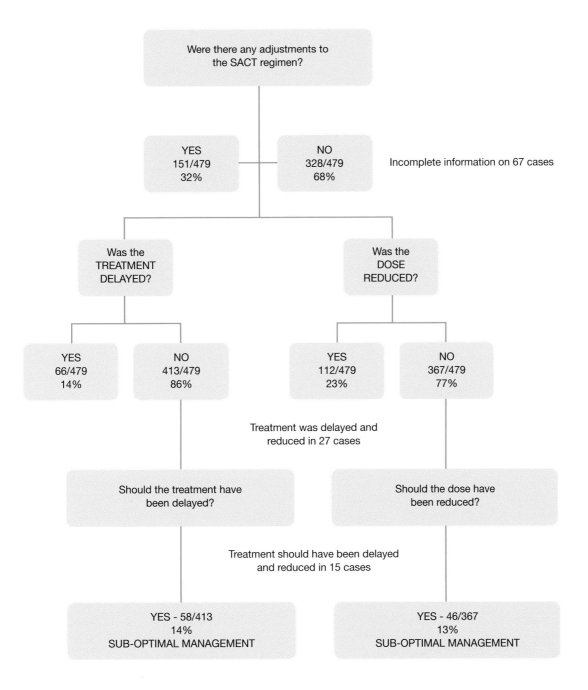

Figure 6.17 Advisors' opinion on SACT doses and timing

Key findings

96% of hospitals provide written information to patients about what to do if they become unwell (247/256 for clinical/medical oncology and 237/248 for haemato-oncology).

43% (220/514) of cases who died within 30 days of SACT suffered grade 3/4 treatment related toxicity.

1 in 5 hospitals did not have a policy for the emergency admission of patients with SACT toxicity (23% (60/258) clinical/medical oncology and 19% (46/244) for haemato-oncology).

The last cycle of SACT was given at a reduced dose in 23% (112/479) of cases. In the advisors' opinion a further 13% (46/367) of cases should have had a reduced dose of SACT.

The last cycle of SACT was delayed in 14% (66/479) of cases. In the advisors' opinion a further 14% (58/413) of cases should have had the administration of SACT delayed.

In the advisors' opinion 12% (51/435) of patients continued to receive SACT when there was obvious disease progression.

Recommendations

If the patient has suffered clinically significant grade 3/4 toxicity with the previous cycle of SACT, a dose reduction or the use of prophylactic GCSF should be considered depending on the treatment intent. *(Consultants and clinical directors)*

Consultants should follow good clinical practice and consider:
- Reducing the dose of SACT in patients
  - that have received a number of previous courses of treatment
  - that have a poor performance status
  - that have significant co-morbidity;
- Reducing the dose of or omitting drugs excreted via the kidney, if the patient has impaired renal function;
- Reducing the dose of or omitting drugs excreted via the liver, if the patient has impaired liver function. *(Consultants and clinical directors)*

7 – Hospital admissions during the last 30 days of life

Introduction

Although the majority of patients in this study were treated with palliative intent, it is entirely appropriate that they were admitted to hospital for the management of acute complications of treatment. Having accepted the risks associated with SACT, patients have every right to expect that they will receive care of the highest standard should they develop complications. In this chapter the process of care of patients who were admitted to hospital but died within 30 days of receiving SACT is examined.

Patients were selected for the study because they had died within 30 days of receiving SACT. Of the 659 patients for whom a questionnaire B was completed, 557 (85%) were admitted to hospital during the last 30 days of life. In 82% of these cases (473/557), patients were admitted to the hospital in which they had received SACT.

Admission of patients during the last 30 days of life by hospital type

Table 7.1 Admissions by hospital type

Ward	Type of hospital				
	Cancer Centre	NHSUni TeachHosp	NHSDist GenHosp	Independent	Total
Oncology	131	24	20	2	177
Haemato-oncology	27	23	16	0	66
General haematology	0	2	10	0	12
General medicine	62	11	65	1	139
MAU	24	4	15	0	43
General surgery	9	0	9	0	18
ICU/ITU/HDU	2	2	1	0	5
Palliative care	6	3	4	0	13
Other	20	4	14	0	38
Subtotal	281	73	154	3	511
Unknown	18	1	11	0	30
Total	299	74	165	3	541

*Denominator drops to 541 as data were obtained from questionnaire B and Organisational questionnaire.

From Table 7.1 it can be seen that compared with those admitted to distinct general hospitals (DGHs), patients admitted to cancer centres and NHS teaching hospitals were more likely to be admitted under the care of a specialist oncology team because this is where there are greater concentrations of oncology staff and oncology beds. The DGH's that can admit directly to an oncology specialist are likely to be those defined by the JCCO as type 1 cancer units that have a requirement to have a consultant oncology on-call rota.

Nevertheless, even in cancer centres and NHS teaching hospitals many patients were admitted as general medical emergencies in the first instance. Of the 557 patients admitted to hospital, similar numbers were admitted to the specialties of general medicine and general haematology as were admitted under the care of an oncologist or haemato-oncologist.

Specialty of first admission during last 30 days of life
Figure 7.1 demonstrates the specialty under whose care the patient was admitted. While the oncology specialties take almost half of these admissions, a heavy burden falls on general medicine.

From questionnaire B it could be seen that 252 patients were admitted under the care of an oncologist or haemato-oncologist but a further 239 patients were admitted under general medicine, a medical assessment unit or haematology. Only 12 patients were admitted under the care of a palliative care consultant and five were admitted directly to a critical care bed.

For patients admitted as emergencies with medical conditions not directly related to SACT, admission under the care of a specialty other than oncology or haemato-oncology would be appropriate. The question is, whether or not patients with complications of SACT should be managed solely by the specialist oncology services?

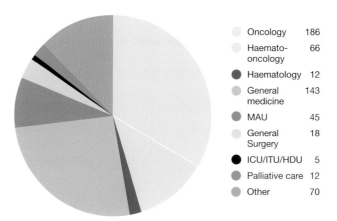

Oncology	186
Haemato-oncology	66
Haematology	12
General medicine	143
MAU	45
General Surgery	18
ICU/ITU/HDU	5
Palliative care	12
Other	70

Figure 7.1 Specialty of first admission during last 30 days of life

The admission of many patients to general medicine in this study stands out. This reflects the fact that oncology services are not yet abundant enough to provide emergency cover in all hospitals that may admit patients with complications of SACT. As with many other specialties there is sometimes a conflict between providing a service only in a limited number of centres to which the patient must travel, or providing the service nearer to the patient's home and accepting that the full range of back up available in the centre might not be readily accessible. Oncology services have developed a hub and spoke approach, with radiotherapy and the treatment of some rare cancers being available only in specialist centres but with SACT for the more common cancers being available in hospitals acting as cancer units closer to the patient's home. The service as presently configured does not have the number of staff or the bed base to manage the admission of all patients who become unwell after SACT even in the larger centres. According to a recent census of consultant physicians in the UK[24] in 1993 there were just 76 medical oncologists for the whole of England Wales and Northern Ireland. This rose to 150 by 2001 and there are now at least 197 in England alone while Wales has 5. This is in addition to haematologists who have sub-specialised in the treatment of haematological malignancies, and clinical oncologists who deliver SACT as well as radiotherapy.

How patients sought advice when unwell

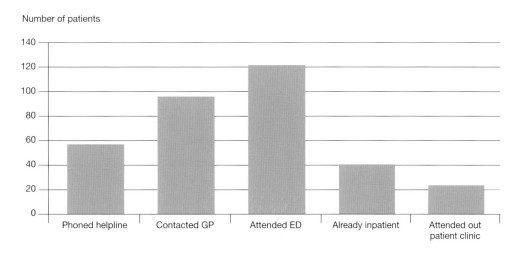

Figure 7.2 Where patients sought advice when unwell

Table 7.2 How help was obtained for those subsequently admitted to hospital

Admitted to hospital	How help was obtained			
	Phoned helpline	Contacted GP	Attended ED	Attended out patient clinic
Yes	55	87	122	23
No	3	8	4	2
Subtotal	58	95	126	25
Not answered	0	2	0	0
Total	58	97	126	25

Although most hospitals had an emergency helpline, it is clear from Figure 7.2 that the majority of patients chose to contact their GP or attend an emergency department (ED). Table 7.2 shows that no matter who they contacted for advice this was an acutely ill patient group and the majority were admitted to hospital.

As well as evidence that patients did not always seek advice in the way expected, it was identified that some patients delayed seeking advice (Figure 7.3). From the data provided it was not possible to determine clearly how long patients delayed reporting their symptoms.

For 53 patients where it was clear there had been a delay it was often short (1-3 days) but even delays of a day can be critical in patients with grade 3/4 toxicity. There were examples of patients delaying for up to 2 weeks. It is of course possible that they sought advice from other sources besides the hospital, in which case such advice might have delayed their admission and treatment. Forty three patients delayed seeking advice for at least 24 hours after the onset of a grade 3/4 event. For some patients the system put in place to ensure that they are promptly assessed when they become unwell failed.

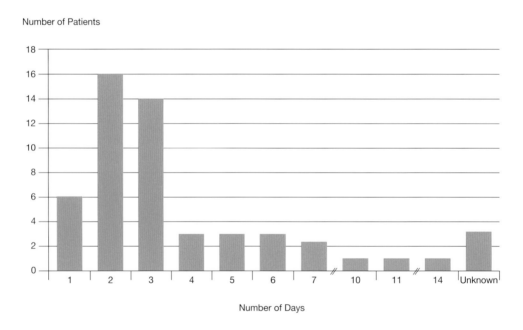

Figure 7.3 Delay of patients reporting grade 3/4 toxicity

Case study 9

History

A patient receiving palliative SACT delayed reporting symptoms of diarrhoea, vomiting and fever for 2 days. By this time they were in renal failure. The patient's condition was compounded by lack of effective medical treatment of hypotension after admission.

Problems noted by the advisors

- The medical team did not seem to recognise how serious the toxicity was
- Although the SACT was palliative the complications were potentially treatable
- The patient presented too late and received less than good care.

In summary, this study has demonstrated that, despite patients being given advice on how and when to seek help, the advice is not always followed. And whether followed or not, many patients will be admitted as general medical emergencies. It is vitally important that mechanisms are put into place in every hospital so that clinicians admitting patients with complications of SACT have access to sufficient patient details that appropriate decisions can be made. This could be addressed to some extent by service level agreements between hospitals within cancer networks. Such agreements might include speed at which oncologists are informed of a patient's admission, access to specialist advice and patient management plans, advice on triage of patients for admission, and training in the recognition and treatment of complications of SACT.

Appropriateness of the specialty for patient's condition

The local clinician completing questionnaire B was asked whether they thought the admission had been to an acceptable specialty. Very few thought that the admission was to an inappropriate specialty (22/546) and in 11 cases this was not answered. The result was similar when the advisors were asked the same question (31/402 that could be assessed). This pattern of addmission may simply be due to that fact that it is the current accepted practice, and general physicians may have the beds to admit these patients. However, in some of the advisor group meetings, the expert group meeting, and at the NCEPOD steering group meeting there was considerable discussion about whether doctors managing general medical emergency admissions would be as well placed to recognise the complications of SACT and treat these patients as specialist oncology staff and whether it was appropriate that general medicine should carry the burden of treating SACT patients that become unwell following treatment.

"It is entirely reasonable that a physician on call for the general medical take should be able to manage neutropenic sepsis. It is part of training for all physicians"
(Quote from an advisors' meeting)

"Patients with complications directly due to SACT should be admitted under the care of oncologists who have the specialist knowledge necessary to care for them. The oncologist is also more likely to know when further intervention is futile"
(Quote from an advisors' meeting)

Concerns centred mostly on general physicians not having access to the patient's notes especially when admitted to a hospital other than the one in which SACT had been given. Delay in recognising and initiating treatment of neutropenic sepsis was a topic that came up frequently in the advisors' meetings as individual cases were discussed. At most meetings examples were found where patients should have commenced antibiotics earlier.

It is evident that general medicine presently provides a substantial part of the emergency care of patients admitted following SACT, and as long as it does so there will be a need for continuing education in the recognition and treatment of complications arising in these patients. Alternatively there needs to be a change in the current system so that the patients can be referred quickly to an oncologist.

Time to review by an oncologist/haemato-oncologist

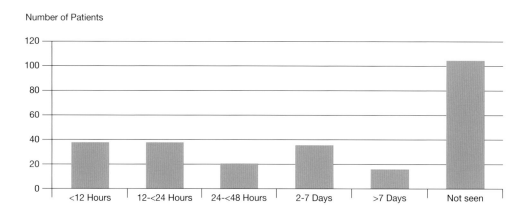

Figure 7.4 Time to review by oncology/haemoto-oncology team

For patients not admitted directly under the care of an oncology or haemato-oncology team, Figure 7.4 illustrates the time taken for the patient to be seen by a member of the oncology/haemato-oncology team, whether or not they had already seen a consultant from another specialty.

Because not all hospitals admitting patients with complications of SACT have oncology services on site there are likely to be further delays before the patient is seen by a consultant oncologist in these hospitals. It is also clear that some patients were never reviewed by an oncology/haemato-oncology team, although that is not to say that specialist advice was not obtained in some other way or that such a consultation would necessarily have altered the outcome.

Management of SACT complications

All treatment with SACT is associated with some risk of side effects. Organisations should have written clinical care guidelines on how to manage the commonest problems. These policies should be easily accessible to clinical staff caring for patients with SACT toxicity and other complications.

STANDARDS

Networks should agree, document and disseminate guidelines for both prophylaxis and management of neutropenic sepsis. Patients, their carers, primary care teams, accident and emergency departments, and others who may encounter this type of problem should be given precise information about whom they should contact and where patients should be taken in the event of treatment complications. These patients should be managed by a specialist haemato-oncology MDT.
Improving outcomes in haematological cancer: NICE 2003[7]

Every acute hospital should have written guidelines on the diagnosis and management of neutropenic sepsis. All medical staff should be aware of their existence and a copy should be readily available in all relevant clinical areas including Accident & Emergency.

Intravenous antibiotics should be commenced within 30 minutes in 100% of patients who have received recent chemotherapy and who are shocked.
Chemotherapy Guidelines: COIN 2001[2]

Every acute hospital should have written guidelines on the use and role of Growth Factors in the management of bone marrow suppression and neutropenic sepsis secondary to cytotoxic chemotherapy. All medical staff should be aware of their existence and a copy should be readily available in all relevant clinical areas including Accident & Emergency.
Chemotherapy Guidelines: COIN 2001[2]

Analysis of the data from the 295 completed organisational questionnaires revealed that the policies shown in Table 7.3 were available.

Table 7.3 Policies available

	Yes (%)	No (%)	Subtotal	Not answered	Total
Management of neutropenic sepsis	266 (94)	17 (6)	**283**	12	**295**
Anti-emetics	251 (89)	31 (11)	**282**	13	**295**
Prophylactic antibiotics	210 (78)	59 (22)	**269**	26	**295**
The use of growth factors	210 (77)	63 (23)	**273**	22	**295**

The study found that the policies were stored in the sites shown in Table 7.4.

Table 7.4 Storage of local clinical care policies

	Yes (%)	No (%)	Subtotal	Not answered	Total
Ward areas	227 (91)	23 (9)	250	45	295
Chemotherapy clinic	211 (93)	16 (7)	227	68	295
Electronic version on hospital computers	192 (85)	33 (15)	225	70	295
Outpatient departments	121 (67)	59 (33)	180	115	295
On site library	37 (24)	117 (76)	154	141	295
Included in medical staff induction pack	34 (23)	115 (77)	149	146	295

Whilst most organisations reported that policies on the management of SACT toxicity had been written, review of individual casenotes revealed that staff were not always familiar with their content and that the policies were not always easily accessible.

Grade 3 or 4 toxicity

Analysis of the data from the assessment forms revealed that 250/444 patients suffered a grade 3/4 event within 30 days of their most recent SACT (in 102 cases it was unknown, Table 7.5).

Table 7.5 Grade 3 or 4 event following last cycle of SACT

Grade 3 or 4 toxicity	Number of patients (%)
Yes	250 (56)
Not documented	194 (44)
Subtotal	444
Unknown	102
Total	546

These events were managed in the following ways:
- Antibiotics (107)
- GCSF (26)
- Blood transfusion
- Anticoagulants
- Anti-emetics
- Loperamide
- Allopurinol
- Bisphosphonates
- Digoxin
- Assisted respiration

In the opinion of the advisors the management of the toxicity was appropriate in 126/141 cases, inappropriate in 15/141 cases and was not assessed in 109/250 cases.

Inappropriate management included:
- Oral antibiotics in the treatment of high risk neutropenic sepsis;
- No gentamicin or gram negative cover in a patient with severe neutropenic sepsis;
- Delay in commencing antibiotics;
- Standard doses of gentamicin in the presence of renal failure.

Case study 10

History

An elderly patient with liver metastases from a lung cancer had received treatment with SACT. After feeling unwell for 2 days the patient attended an emergency department. The patient had a high temperature 39.5C, and a low blood pressure 75/40. No neutropenic sepsis policy was available in the emergency department; the cancer centre was contacted and a copy of the policy was faxed over. This resulted in a delay of 2 hours in commencing antibiotics. The patient was transferred to a general medicine bed 12 hours after arrival in the emergency department and died 6 hours later.

Problems noted by the advisors

- Delay in patient seeking advice when unwell
- No neutropenic policy in the emergency department
- Delay in starting antibiotics
- Delay in admission to a general medical ward.

Neutropenic sepsis

Neutropenic sepsis is a potentially life threatening complication of SACT and as such must be investigated and treated in a department which has a policy for the emergency treatment required and criteria for transfer to an intensive care unit if necessary. The acute management of this condition should be included in the training of all junior doctors.

Local policies

All hospitals administering SACT or accepting emergency admissions should have a local clinical care protocol for the management of this complication and in fact the majority did. Only 17/283 (6%) hospitals had no policy, of which 16 were independent hospitals (Table 7.6).

Case study 11

History

A very elderly patient was receiving SACT for lung cancer. After the third cycle there was documented evidence of neutropenia. The patient was not reviewed by a consultant and a further cycle of SACT was commenced. The patient died soon after from neutropenic sepsis.

Problems noted by the advisors

- Many examples of poor management of neutropenia
- Investigation results were not acted on
- No senior review was obtained.

Table 7.6 Management of neutropenic sepsis policy available

Management of neutropenic sepsis policy	Number of hospitals (%)
Yes	266 (94)
No	17 (6)
Subtotal	**283**
Not answered	12
Total	**295**

Information from the local clinician completing questionnaire B revealed that 16% (83/514) of patients suffered febrile neutropenia.

Hospital admissions

All 83 patients with neutropenic sepsis were admitted to hospital. Nine patients were planned admissions to haemato-oncology wards (6), general medical ward (1) or an unknown ward type (2). The 74 emergency admissions were admitted to oncology (21), haemato-oncology (13), general medicine (15), and a medical assessment unit (16) another type of ward type (6) or critical care (3).

Table 7.7 shows that whilst most of the 74 acute admissions with neutropenic sepsis were shared between the oncology and medical services, many patients were eventually transferred to more specialist units.

Table 7.7 Where patients died following admission		
Admitted to	**Died**	
Oncology/haemato-oncology	Oncology/haemato-oncology	22
	Home	2
	Hospice	1
	Critical care	7
	Not answered	2
General medicine	Oncology/haemato-oncology	6
	Medical ward	4
	Palliative ward	1
	Other	2
	Not answered	2
Medical assessment unit	Oncology/haemato-oncology	5
	Medical ward	2
	Home	1
	Critical care	3
	Other	3
	Not answered	2
Critical care	Critical care	3
Other	Oncology/haemato-oncology	2
	Critical care	2
	Not answered	1
	Other	1

Clinical management of neutropenic sepsis

STANDARDS
Empirical intravenous antibiotic therapy must be initiated immediately for patients satisfying the criteria for neutropenic sepsis.

Intravenous antibiotics should be commenced within 30 minutes in 100% of patients who have received recent chemotherapy and who are shocked.
Chemotherapy Guidelines: COIN 2001[2]

Seventy eight out of 83 patients were treated according to the local protocol. Information was not available for two patients and 3/83 patients were considered by the local clinician to have had suboptimal care. The deaths of these three patients were a direct result of a SACT complication and in two cases delay in treatment of the toxicity was a contributing factor to the death.

Of these cases of neutropenic sepsis 18/83 were discussed at an audit or morbidity and mortality meeting. It is important that all treatment related deaths are reviewed and reported to clinical governance committees. Following local review, further staff education on the management of neutropenic sepsis was initiated in one organisation and a clinical care pathway written in another.

Retrospective review of neutropenic sepsis cases by the local clinicians caring for the patient at the time of death (questionnaire B) and the advisory panel highlighted the following problem areas:

Organisational aspects
- No neutropenic policy in emergency departments;
- Clinicians unaware of the neutropenic sepsis policy;
- Inappropriate place of care for a patient with a serious complication of chemotherapy – e.g. a medical assessment unit, general medical ward, ENT ward;
- Difficulties as the oncologist only visits the cancer unit once a week.

Clinical aspects
- Failure of junior doctors to make the diagnosis;
- Lack of early assessment by senior medical staff;
- Delay in admission to hospital;
- Unacceptable delay in resuscitation;
- Unacceptable delay in prescribing antibiotics – 4 hours;
- Unacceptable delay in administration of antibiotics – 12 hours after prescription written;
- Unacceptable delay in senior staff review;
- Unacceptable delay in transfer to intensive care;
- Different antibiotics used to those stated in the local policy;
- Lack of staff awareness that patients may not always have a fever with neutropenic sepsis.

Patient factors
- Patient information should stress the continuing risk of sepsis even after completion of last cycle of chemotherapy.
- Patients not following protocols to obtain advice when they became unwell.

Case study 12

History

A patient with stage IV Hodgkin's disease was admitted with a two day history of diarrhoea, 8 days following the third cycle of chemotherapy. The patient was dehydrated and had a low blood pressure 80/50 and a raised temperature 38.5C. The patient was reviewed by an SHO on admission and a clinical diagnosis of pneumonia was made. 12 hours later the patient was assessed by a registrar, commenced on intravenous antibiotics and transferred to ITU.

Problems noted by the advisors

- Delay in diagnosis and treatment of septic shock in a patient with a potentially curable malignancy
- Lack of early assessment by senior medical staff.

Case study 13

History

A middle aged patient with liver and lung metastases was planned to commence SACT. Full blood count, renal and liver function test were satisfactory. The treatment commenced after a 3 weeks holiday and 3 days later the patient was admitted with back pain and general malaise. On examination the patient had a raised temperature 39C, was jaundiced and drowsy. Intravenous antibiotics and GCSF were started 24 hours after admission following review by the consultant. The temperature settled and neutrophil count recovered but the patient died from liver failure due to progressive disease.

Problems noted by the advisors

- No clinical review immediately prior to SACT – patient's condition had deteriorated
- No LFT test immediately prior to chemotherapy
- Delay in diagnosis and treatment of septic shock
- Lack of early assessment by senior medical staff.

Key findings

239/557 (42%) patients were admitted to general medicine following a SACT complication rather than to oncology/haemato-oncology specialists.

17/281 (6%) hospitals had no policy for the management of neutropenic sepsis.

17% (43/250) of patients who had a grade 3/4 event delayed seeking advice for at least 24 hours.

Recommendations

A debate within the profession is needed to explore whether it is appropriate that patients treated with SACT should be admitted under general medicine if problems occur. Any substantial change would require expansion of the oncology workforce. An alternative would be a strengthening of links between oncology and general medicine to ensure protocols and training are in place for the management of complications of SACT. *(Medical directors, cancer services managers and clinical directors)*

Emergency admissions services must have the resources to manage SACT toxicity. These should include:
- A clinical care pathway for suspected neutropenic sepsis;
- A local policy for the management of neutropenic sepsis;
- Appropriately trained staff familiar with the neutropenic sepsis policy;
- The policy should be easily accessible in all emergency departments;
- Availability of appropriate antibiotics within the emergency department. *(Cancer services managers and clinical directors)*

In planning the provision of oncology services outside of cancer centres, commissioners should take into account the need for specialist advice to be readily available when patients are admitted acutely. *(Cancer services managers)*

8 – End of life care

"How we care for the dying is an indicator of how we care for all sick and vulnerable people. It is a measure of society as a whole and it is a litmus test for health and social care services."

(Quote from End of Life Care Strategy DH 2008)[25]

Palliative care services

Palliative care teams should be involved according to the individual patient's needs, especially when they have unpleasant symptoms that are proving difficult to control.

Of the 546 cases reviewed by the advisors, it was apparent that advice from the palliative care team was given for just 157 patients. Oncologists are trained in the care of terminally ill patients but specialist palliative care support has a role in many patients receiving palliative SACT, especially those who have relapsed after previous treatments – a group very evident in this study.

SACT was given with palliative intent in 85% (557/649) of patients in this study. However, there was very little documentation regarding advanced consideration of the patient's wishes in the event of sudden deterioration in their condition. It is possible that this could lead to confusion about the appropriate measures to be taken when such patients are admitted as emergencies, especially under the care of clinicians not usually involved in their care such as general physicians.

End of life care

The end of life care strategy is one of eight clinical pathways developed by each of the Strategic Health Authorities in England as part of Lord Darzi's NHS Next Stage Review[23]. It attempts to provide the first comprehensive framework aimed at promoting high quality care for adults approaching the end of life.

"During the development of the end of life strategy many people have identified the lack of open discussion between health care staff and those approaching the end of life, as one of the key barriers to the delivery of good end of life care.

This represents a major challenge. It requires a significant culture shift both amongst the public and within the NHS. Clinicians and managers need to accept that death does not always represent a failure of healthcare and that enabling people to die as well as possible is one of the core functions of the NHS."

(Quote from End of Life Care Strategy DH 2008)[25]

NCEPOD strongly supports the use of an end of life pathway when managing patients in their last days of life. For example the Liverpool care pathway was originally developed for use with cancer patients. Such a tool was identified in the casenotes of 57 patients in this study. Since the notes of 304 patients contained a do not attempt resuscitation (DNAR) statement, it appeared that such a pathway could have been implemented for many more patients. A recent report on end of life strategy anticipated that only 17% of acute trusts would have implemented such a tool on all appropriate wards by January 2008[25].

Case study 14

History
A middle aged patient declined treatment for a haematological malignancy. There was a two day delay starting an end of life pathway because of what were described as ward and staffing difficulties. The patient died half an hour after staff agreed to commence the pathway.

Problems noted by the advisors
- A decision to offer palliative care rather than treatment with SACT had been made but the team did not work in the patient's best interest
- The delay in starting the end of life pathway was unacceptable.

A change in the behaviour of health professionals towards patients who have incurable cancer and who are dying is needed. A recent report commissioned by the Royal College of Physicians of London)[29] found that referrals to palliative care services were often made late when patients had multiple problems and significant distress. NCEPOD supports the recommendation of this report that generic palliative care should be a core part of

training for all healthcare professionals and a requirement for continuing professional development (CPD). Patients are unlikely to enter into discussions about advance directives, preferred place of death and the involvement of palliative care services unless they know that these are options and that they have the right to express their preferences.

All health care professionals who deal with people who are dying should have a clear understanding of how to discuss, facilitate and make available these choices. Oncologists are in an ideal position to support the objectives of the end of life strategy by being open and willing to discuss death and dying, especially with patients whose SACT is likely to be palliative. They should also enquire about the patient's preferred place of death. However, if the patient makes it clear that they do not wish to enter into such discussions, their choice must be respected and clearly documented in the casenotes.

Resuscitation status

Decisions regarding the resuscitation status of all patients with cancer should be clearly annotated in the medical record. A DNAR order means that in the event of a cardiac arrest, cardiopulmonary resuscitation would not be attempted. However the patient would continue to have all active treatment necessary for their malignancy, symptoms and any complications arising as a direct result of treatment.

Discussions regarding resuscitation status are held between a senior doctor and the patient and/or relatives. It should not be discussed without the patient's consent unless there are issues of patient capacity to decide.

In 546 cases reviewed by the advisors evidence of a DNAR statement was found in the notes of 304 patients. In 20 cases this had been discussed with the patient alone, and in 39 with the patient and relatives (Figure 8.1). In 143 cases it was discussed with the relatives only.

Number of Cases

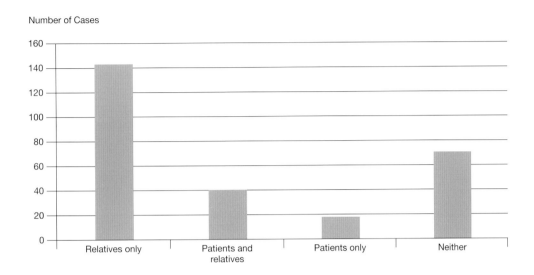

Figure 8.1 Who the DNAR was discussed with

"Clinicians very closely involved in the care of these patients and their families can find it very difficult to know when to stop treatment. Discussion with colleagues or the palliative care team can give a different perspective"
(Quote from an advisor)

"Discussing these patients in an MDT is a waste of time. Only the consultant responsible for the patients' treatment can decide when it is worth continuing treatment"
(Quote from a local clinician)

Place of death

The place of death shown in Figure 8.2 reflects the fact that the majority of patients were cared for by medical and oncology specialties.

117

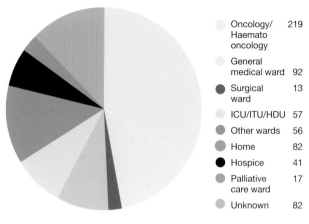

Oncology/ Haemato oncology	219
General medical ward	92
Surgical ward	13
ICU/ITU/HDU	57
Other wards	56
Home	82
Hospice	41
Palliative care ward	17
Unknown	82

Figure 8.2 Where the patients died

Most of the patients in this study were treated with palliative intent. However, for many patients death was unexpected so soon after treatment and therefore a hospital admission was appropriate.

From Figure 7.1 (Chapter 7) it can be seen that 12 patients in this study were admitted directly to a palliative care bed, and from Figure 8.2 it can be seen that an additional 5 patients were transferred to this specialty and 58 patients in total died while in a palliative care bed or hospice.

Number of Patients

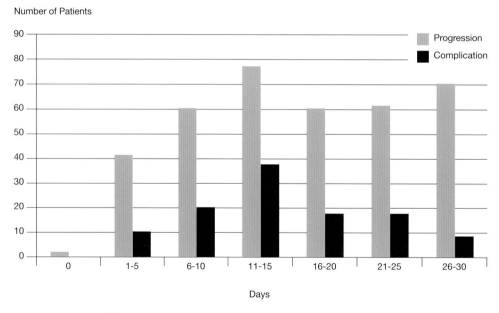

Days

Figure 8.3 Time between first day of SACT and death

Eighty two patients died at home but there were insufficient details on these patients to determine whether they had made a choice to do so or had died at home unexpectedly. Surveys of both the general population and those with a terminal illness suggest that most people would prefer to die at home, yet 56% of all deaths from cancer occur in an acute hospital, with only 20% of patients with cancer dying at home in accordance with their wishes[29].

In 486/557 patients admitted after SACT the interval between the first day of the last cycle of SACT and the date of death could be calculated. Half the deaths occurred within the first 15 days. The peak of deaths at 11-15 days was probably related to the development of neutropenic sepsis.

It can be seen from Figure 8.3 that when the interval between SACT and death of patients was examined, where the advisors considered SACT had contributed to or caused death, the interval follows the pattern of onset of toxicity as would be expected. The interval to death of patients whose deaths were considered to be due to progression of disease continued to rise after 16-20 days.

Critical care beds

STANDARD

If the team caring for the patient considers that admission to a critical care area is clinically indicated, then the decision to admit should involve both the consultant caring for the patient on the ward and the consultant in critical care.
NICE clinical guideline 50[26]

Fifty seven patients died in a critical care bed. Of these, 27 patients had received SACT with curative intent. The cause of death in these patients was treatment related (mainly neutropenic sepsis) (36), progressive disease (9) unrelated to the malignancy (6) and unknown (6).

Cause of death

Solid tumours
Death was unexpected in those patients with solid tumours who received neo-adjuvant SACT (8), adjuvant SACT (10) and definitive potentially curative SACT or chemoradiotherapy (17).

Neo-adjuvant SACT
Eight patients received chemotherapy or chemoradiotherapy prior to planned surgical resection of the primary tumour. The chance of cure in these patients was estimated as >50% (1), 20-49% (5), no data (2). The case was discussed at an MDT meeting in 7 cases. The course of treatment was initiated by a consultant in 7 cases.

Adjuvant SACT
Ten patients received chemotherapy following complete surgical resection of the primary tumour. The chance of cure in these patients was estimated as >50% (4), 20-49% (4), no data (2). The case was discussed at an MDT meeting in 9 cases. The course of treatment was initiated by a consultant in 10 cases.

Potentially curable
Eleven patients with solid tumours received chemotherapy or chemo-radiotherapy as potentially curative treatment for a solid tumour. The chance of cure in these patients was estimated as >50% (2), 20-49% (4), no data (5). The case was discussed at an MDT meeting in all 11 cases. The course of treatment was initiated by a consultant in all cases.

Haematological malignancies

Fifty four patients received potentially curative treatment for haematological malignancies. These included 14 cases of acute leukaemia, 38 cases of lymphoma and two unknown. The chance of cure in these patients was estimated as >50% (8), 20-49% (23), no data (23). The case was discussed at an MDT meeting in only 11 cases. The course of treatment was initiated by a consultant in 52 cases. The lymphomas were treated with RCHOP (20), CHOP (6), and other regimens (12). The acute leukaemias were treated with DA daunorubicin, cytosine (7), UKALLXII clinical trial (2), FLAG (2) and other regimens (3).

Effect of treatment on outcome

In the absence of an autopsy on each case to confirm the findings at death, advisors were asked to give an opinion as to whether they believed SACT had had a direct effect on the patient's outcome. The majority of patients in this study received palliative SACT so in the majority progression of disease was considered to be the cause of death. However, in 27% (115/429) of cases the advisors believed that the SACT caused or hastened death (Figure 8.4). Cases where the death was a direct result of the treatment given should have been referred to HM Coroner, as an autopsy would have clarified the cause of death and an inquest held if necessary. The study data did not reveal how many cases were discussed with a coroner however post mortem examinations were only carried out on 4% of cases.

This was a substantial number of patients that died from the effects of the SACT. When making the decision to treat with SACT an assessment of risk versus benefit must be made. In these cases the risk was either known or it was wrongly assessed. For these patients who died from the effects of the SACT, end of life care could have been improved if they had not received the treatment.

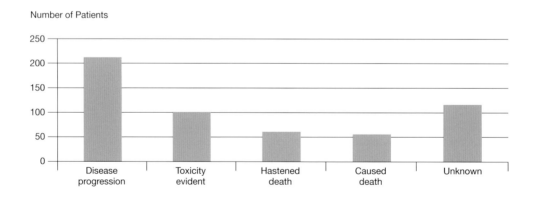

Figure 8.4 Effect of treatment on outcome

120

Audit/clinical governance

STANDARDS

Participation in audit is a contractual requirement for doctors. Audit should be both medical and clinical, regular and systematic. In May 1993 the Conference of Medical Royal Colleges (now Academy of Medical Royal Colleges) recommended that doctors should spend the equivalent of one half session per week on audit activities, including not only the formal meetings but the work required in collecting and analysing data and documentation. Departmental meetings should take place at least once per month. There should be enthusiastic participation by all those concerned. A programme should be published in advance and there should be a register of attendance. Clerical staff should be available to assist with the collection and collation of information
Good Practice Guide for Clinical Oncologists: The Royal College of Radiologists 2003[18]

The medical oncologist must participate in regular and systematic medical and clinical audit. Topics for audit must include specific aspects of medical practice including the outcomes of systemic therapy with respect to both benefits and side-effects of treatment.
Good Medical Practice for Physicians. Royal College of Physicians of London 2004[27]

Compliance with local guidelines for management of neutropenic sepsis and treatment outcomes should be regularly audited and the guidelines should be regularly reviewed.
Chemotherapy Guidelines Clinical Oncology: The Royal College of Radiologists 2001[2]

Patient management/clinical audit

The majority of hospitals reported that regular audit/clinical governance meetings were held.

Table 8.1 Audit meetings held

	Regular audit/governance meetings				
Type	Yes	No	Subtotal	Not answered	Total
Cancer Centre	48	0	48	2	50
NHSUniTeachHosp	28	2	30	3	33
NHSDistGenHosp	107	11	118	7	125
Independent	60	10	70	8	78
NHSOther	5	0	5	4	9
Total	248	23	271	24	295

It can be seen from Table 8.1 that 92% (248/271) of hospitals reported that regular meetings were held, but, as can be seen from Tables 8.2 and 8.3 many did not include formal audit of complications and deaths of patients receiving SACT.

Table 8.2 Audit topics discussed in patients with solid tumours

Audit topic	Yes (%)	No (%)	Subtotal	Not answered	Total
Chemotherapy toxicity	55 (26)	156 (74)	**211**	84	**295**
Neutropenic sepsis	101 (45)	123 (55)	**224**	71	**295**
Nausea and vomiting	47 (23)	161 (77)	**208**	87	**295**
Adherence to NICE guidance	107 (51)	104 (49)	**211**	84	**295**
Efficacy of SACT	27 (15)	159 (85)	**186**	109	**295**
Deaths within 30 days	47 (24)	151 (76)	**198**	97	**295**
Deaths within 60 days	24 (12)	172 (88)	**196**	99	**295**

Table 8.3 Audit topics discussed in patients with haematological malignancies

Audit topic	Yes (%)	No (%)	Subtotal	Not answered	Total
Chemotherapy toxicity	39 (21)	148 (79)	**187**	108	**295**
Neutropenic sepsis	100 (51)	96 (49)	**196**	99	**295**
Nausea and vomiting	37 (20)	147 (80)	**184**	111	**295**
Adherence to NICE guidance	102 (55)	83 (45)	**185**	110	**295**
Efficacy of SACT	27 (16)	140 (84)	**167**	128	**295**
Deaths within 30 days	24 (14)	145 (86)	**169**	126	**295**
Deaths within 60 days	11 (7)	158 (93)	**169**	126	**295**

Medical and clinical oncologists audited deaths within 30 days of SACT in only 47 hospitals, and audited neutropenic sepsis in 101 (Table 8.2). Haemato-oncologists audited deaths within 30 days in 24 hospitals and neutropenic sepsis in 100 (Table 8.3).

Whether or not the patient's death had been discussed at an audit or morbidity and mortality meeting was assessed. In only 76/485 (16%) cases in this study were discussed (Table 8.4).

Table 8.4 Death discussed at a morbidity and mortality meeting

Death discussed at M&M meeting	Number of patients (%)
Yes	76 (16
No	409 (84
Subtotal	**485**
Unknown	139
Not answered	3
Total	**659**

Table 8.5 Case discussed at morbidity and mortality meeting by treatment intent

	Case discussed at a M&M meeting				
Type	Yes	No	Subtotal	Not answered	Tota
Potentially curative	18	37	55	14	69
Adjuvant	1	4	5	8	33
Neo-adjuvant	0	5	5	1	6
High dose palliative	1	13	14	5	19
Palliative	45	315	360	128	488
Subtotal	**65**	**374**	**439**	**156**	**595**
Unknown	1	3	4	4	8
Total	**66**	**377**	**443**	**160**	**603**

Denominator drops as data are taken from questionnaire A and questionnaire B.

In addition the data were examined to see which patients were discussed at morbidity and mortality meetings. Table 8.5 shows that if a patient was treated with potentially curative intent they were more likely to have been discussed than a patient treated with palliative intent. However, looking specifically at patients who received adjuvant, neo-adjuvant or high dose palliative SACT, relatively few were discussed. Discussion of these groups would probably be informative. Similarly, less than a quarter of patients whose death was thought to be a consequence of treatment rather than disease progression were discussed.

Patients who received SACT under the care of haemato-oncology were more likely to de discussed at a morbidity and mortality meeting (27%) than patients under the care of oncologists specialising in the solid tumours (10%).

NCEPOD has commented previously on the decline in the number of autopsies now performed in patients who die in hospital. Of the 659 patients in this study only 25 were known to have had an autopsy post-mortem. Four of these patients died at home.

For doctors to improve the care for future patients, all cases should be discussed at morbidity and mortality meetings. It allows standards of care to be monitored and audited[30]. Audits are valuable for monitoring practice and, where the chances of response to multiple lines of treatment are low, the results will facilitate a more informed discussion about the mortality rate following SACT. This will help patients to weigh the risks of treatment against the benefits as currently the only formal monitoring of the frequency of SACT-related deaths, in the UK, is in the context of clinical trials. In these cases a highly selected group of patients have been chosen, as they fit the entry criteria for a trial. They will not be representative of the population as a whole.

Key findings

In 27% (115/429) of cases the advisors believed that the SACT had caused death or hastened death.

Cases of neutropenic sepsis in patients with solid tumours were audited in only 45% (101/224) hospitals and in haematological malignancies it was audited in 51% (100/196).

Medical and clinical oncologists audited deaths within 30 days of SACT in only 47 hospitals and haemato-oncologists audited deaths within 30 days in only 24 hospitals.

Only 16% (76/485) of cases who died within 30 days of SACT were discussed at a morbidity and mortality meeting.

Recommendations

A pro-active rather than reactive approach should be adopted to ensure that palliative care treatments or referrals are initiated early and appropriately. Oncologists should enquire at an appropriate time, about any advance decisions the patient might wish to make should they lose the capacity to make their own decisions in the future. *(Consultants)*

Regular clinical audit should be undertaken on the management of all cases of neutropenic sepsis following the administration of SACT. The process of care should be compared to standards agreed by the cancer network. Cancer centres and cancer units should collaborate in undertaking these audits. *(Clinical directors)*

All deaths within 30 days of SACT should be considered at a morbidity and mortality or a clinical governance meeting. *(Clinical directors and consultants)*

9 – Summary of organisational and clinical aspects of care provided

Introduction

The consultant oncologist or haemato-oncologist (questionnaire A) and the consultant clinician responsible for the patient's care at the time of death (questionnaire B) were asked to comment on any organisational or clinical aspects of care that might have had a negative effect on the patient's outcome. The group of advisors were also asked to comment on the standards of care provided for individual cases. Furthermore each hospital was asked to identify any problem areas within their organisation with regard to the care of patients receiving systemic anti-cancer therapy (SACT).

Detailed review of the case records of the patients who died within 30 days of SACT revealed that there was room for improvement in the care provided. Deficiencies in the service were related both to organisational and clinical aspects of care and have been highlighted throughout this report.

This chapter aims to summarise some of the themes that arose during the study.

These should not be interpreted either as findings or recommendations but simply as concerns and issues raised by both the local clinicians and the NCEPOD advisors

Organisational aspects of care

Deficiencies in organisational aspects of care were identified by consultants completing questionnaire A, by consultants completing questionnaire B and by the advisors reviewing the casenotes. The following problem areas were identified:

Limited oncologist and haemato-oncologist presence within DGHs

Clinicians working in non-specialist organisations believed that there was a need for a greater oncology and haemato-oncology presence in their hospitals, that communication with their specialist colleagues was sometimes poor and that the lack of availability of oncology and haemato-oncology notes at the time of the patients' emergency admission was detrimental to the care provided.

Staffing issues within cancer units
- No oncologist at organisation;
- Insufficient oncologist/haemato-oncologist time in cancer units;
- No resident oncologist/haemato-oncologist out of hours;
- Insufficient oncology services within cancer units – patients are cared for in non specialist areas as there is no oncology ward and no full time oncologist.

"Patients in this network are admitted to their local hospital for the management of medical complications of treatment and symptomatic management of cancer. Visits by oncologists are weekly"

Communication issues
- Poor communication between trusts;
- Lack of availability of oncology/haemato-oncology medical records within cancer units and district general hospitals;
- No centralised IT system.

125

"The use of separate notes by the oncology centre makes management by acute physicians more difficult through limited information"

"SACT and other oncology notes are not held at the DGH and are not available to us. Communication with oncologists in relation to in-patients is effectively non-existent"

Place of admission of patients suffering SACT toxicity

Patients suffering side effects from SACT were occasionally admitted to district general hospitals or organisations where there was no 24 hour oncology or haemato-oncology service.

The reasons for admission to non specialist centres include:
- Lack of availability of beds in the cancer centres;
- Proximity to the patient's home;
- Patient's attendance at an accident and emergency department.

These patients were often admitted to general medicine or general surgical wards which may not have been equipped to assess and treat the patient appropriately.

Comments received:
- Patients with SACT toxicity should be admitted to the organisation where SACT was administered;
- Patients with SACT toxicity should not be admitted to a general medicine ward;
- Patients with SACT toxicity should not be admitted to a community hospital with GP beds;
- Patients should not be admitted to DGH where there are no oncology/haemato-oncology beds;
- Poor admissions procedure through accident and emergency department.

"Ideally such patients should be admitted under the care of an appropriate specialist rather than to a general medical bed"

"Patient was given chemotherapy by outreach chemotherapy team and admitted under general medicine take to a district general hospital. My view is that all patients under active chemotherapy should be admitted under the care of the service providing the treatment"

"It is not ideal that someone with a chemotherapy related complication is admitted to a busy medical assessment unit"

Clinical policies
- Lack of availability of a policy for the management of neutropenic sepsis within all acute admissions services.

Capacity and demand
- Insufficient capacity on chemotherapy units lead to unacceptable waiting times for treatment;
- Shortage of beds in the cancer centre leads to delays in admission for chemotherapy;
- There are insufficient beds in cancer centres to admit all patients who are neutropenic post chemotherapy;
- Lack of HDU or ITU beds.

"The lack of availability of a bed at the cancer centre led to a delay in commencing chemotherapy. During the waiting period the patient's condition deteriorated. If treatment had commenced earlier, the outcome may have been different"

"Unable to provide an emergency admission bed on the 8 bed oncology ward. Patient was admitted via MAU (general medicine) where delays in antibiotic administration are common"

"Most acute admissions of patients following chemo come to our hospital due to bed shortages in oncology centre. This often means that we do not have immediate access to oncologist's management plans"

"Patient reviewed early by the outreach team, CPAP suggested, it was not possible to transfer patient to CCU/HDU for CPAP as no bed available. Patient's condition deteriorated"

Staffing within cancer centres
- Low nursing staff levels at weekends;
- Lack of tumour site specific nurse specialist.

"Due to funding cuts, we had no cancer nurse specialist at the time this patient was treated. The absence of this post had a negative effect on communication between doctors, nurses, the patient and relatives"

Referral pathways
- Delay in patient self referral with toxicity;
- Delay in referral to an oncologist or haemato-oncologist;
- Discharge planning – delays in the provision of a care package for terminally ill patients.

"The organisation relies on patients or relatives telephoning the chemotherapy department as instructed, if toxicity occurs. This appears not to have happened. A system which included closer supervision in the community would be beneficial"

Drug funding
- Application for funding for high cost drugs delays treatment.

Drug funding problems were highlighted in relation to docetaxol for prostate cancer, temazolamide for glioma, rituximab for lymphoma and velacade for myeloma.

"There was a delay in commencing chemotherapy because of 1) submission of an application for funding 2) delay in access to chemo slot once funding agreed. The patient was less fit when treated and therefore toxicity worse and likelihood of benefit less"

127

Clinical aspects of care

Decision to treat
- The patient's management plan was not discussed at a MDT meeting;
- SACT was given to patients who were terminally ill, had poor performance status and/or significant co-morbidity;
- Clinician's judgement not to give SACT was influenced by patient's young age and family pressure.

Patient information
- The importance of seeking advice on toxicity early was not stressed strongly enough;
- The patient was unaware that toxicity can continue after the last cycle of SACT is completed;
- An up to date consent form was not always available for each course of SACT;
- The consent form did not always contain the following information: outline of benefits, outline of toxicity, mortality risk, drugs to be given and duration of treatment;
- Some clinicians require further education in breaking bad news.

Communication
- Misleading information given to general practitioner;
- Poor communication between organisations – in some cases the oncologist or haemato-oncologist was unaware of the cause of death even in patients who had been treated with curative intent.

Medical records
- Poor documentation within the medical record of risks/benefits of treatment, patient information provided, GP information, communication between health professionals, consent to treatment and toxicity related to previous cycle of SACT;
- Poor filing within the medical record of consent forms and chemotherapy prescriptions;
- The use of separate oncology or haemato-oncology notes leads to poor communication between hospitals and cancer centres. The use of an electronic patient record that could be accessed by all health professions would decrease the risks associated with the care of patients admitted with complications of treatment following SACT administration.

Process of care
- Lack of up to date clinical assessment prior to SACT;
- Failure to undertake all essential pre-treatment investigations;
- Lack of essential pre-treatment investigations within 72 hours of SACT;
- Lack of senior doctor review when patient's condition deteriorated;
- Lack of notice of nurses' comments;
- Lack of documentation of assessment of tumour response and treatment related toxicity.

Patient management
- Delay in diagnosis;
- No histological diagnosis of malignancy;
- Lack of adjustment of SACT dose and schedule in relation to patient's clinical condition;
- SACT regimens that had previously failed to produce a response were repeated;
- SACT was continued in patients with obvious progressive disease – this was a waste of money, gave false hope and a risk of toxicity;
- Poor management of neutropenic sepsis.

End of life care
- Lack of early discussion and documentation of end of life care;
- Lack of early involvement of the palliative care team;
- Lack of transfer of a DNAR order from one hospital to another organisation;
- Lack of autopsy in cases where death was unexpected.

Advisors' assessments

The multidisciplinary team of advisors consisting of oncologists, haemato-oncologists, a palliative care physician, specialist chemotherapy nurses and cancer pharmacists were asked to comment on the overall care provided for individual patients.

Certain aspects of the clinical care and/or organisational aspects of the service provided were considered to be sub-optimal. The care was considered to be less than satisfactory in 8% of cases - several aspects of care were well below acceptable standards.

The problem areas identified by the advisors were as follows:
- An inappropriate decision to treat with SACT;
- An inappropriate decision to continue SACT.

- An adverse event in prescribing;
- An adverse event in dispensing;
- An adverse event in administration.

- Poor communication between patient and clinicians;
- Poor communication between clinicians.

- Delay in admission with toxicity;
- Inappropriate investigation of toxicity;
- Delay in treating toxicity;
- Inappropriate management of toxicity.

The major concerns were the decision to treat poor performance status patients with advanced disease and the management of patients with SACT toxicity.

Key features of cases where treatment was less than satisfactory were:
- Management of neutropenic sepsis;
- Poor decision to treat with SACT when performance status was low and patient had very advanced disease;
- Unacceptable process of care in prescribing the last cycle of SACT.

References

1. Manual for cancer services. 2004. Department of Health. London
http://www.dh.gov.uk/en/Healthcare/NationalService
Frameworks/Cancer/DH_4135595

2. Chemotherapy Guidelines: Clinical Oncology Information Network (COIN). Royal College of Radiologists.
http://www.rcr.ac.uk

3. Principles to underpin the delivery of radiotherapy and chemotherapy services to NHS cancer patients The Joint Collegiate Council for Oncology February 2007
www.rcr.ac.uk/docs/oncology/pdf/
Principlestounderpin.pdf

4. Guidelines on the Management of Acute Myeloid Leukaemia in Adults (2005). British Committee for Standards in Haematology (BCSH). British Society for Haematology.
http://www.b-s-h.org.uk/

5. Cancer Service Guidance: Improving Outcomes in Cancer. National Institute for Health and Clinical Excellence.
http://www.nice.org.uk/

6. Guidance on the use of ultrasound locating devices for placing central venous catheters Technology Appraisal No. 49 Issue date: September 2002
www.nice.org.uk/nicemedia/pdf/Ultrasound_49_
GUIDANCE.pdf

7. Improving Outcomes in Haematological Cancers The Manual Published by the National Institute for Clinical Excellence October 2003 ISBN:1-84257-398-5
http://www.nice.org.uk/nicemedia/pdf/NICE_
HAEMATOLOGICAL_CSG.pdf

8. Emergency Admissions: A journey in the right direction? 2007. National Confidential Enquiry into Patient Outcome and Death. London.
http://www.ncepod.org.uk/reports.htm

9. The Heart of the Matter. 2008. National Confidential Enquiry into Patient Outcome and Death. London.
http://www.ncepod.org.uk/reports.htm

10. Good medical practice. 2006. General Medical Council. London
http://www.gmc-uk.org/guidance/good_medical_
practice/index.asp

11. Scoping our practice. 2004. National Confidential Enquiry into Patient Outcome and Death. London.
http://www.ncepod.org.uk/reports.htm

12. An acute problem? 2005. National Confidential Enquiry into Patient Outcome and Death. London.
http://www.ncepod.org.uk/reports.htm

13. A service in need of surgery? 2005. National Confidential Enquiry into Patient Outcome and Death. London.
http://www.ncepod.org.uk/reports.htm

14. Trauma: Who cares? 2007. National Confidential Enquiry into Patient Outcome and Death. London.
http://www.ncepod.org.uk/reports.htm

15. A Sickle Crisis? 2008. National Confidential Enquiry into Patient Outcome and Death. London. http://www.ncepod.org.uk/reports.htm

16. Calman Hine report: A policy framework for commissioning cancer services. 1995. Department of Health. London. http://www.dh.gov.uk/en/Publicationsandstatistics/Publications/PublicationsPolicyAndGuidance/DH_4071083

17. Resuscitation council (UK). 2004 (revised 2008). Cardiopulmonary Resuscitation - Standards for clinical practice and training. London. http://www.resus.org.uk/pages/standard.pdf

18. Good Practice Guide for Clinical Oncologists Second edition The Royal College of Radiologists (2003) www.rcr.ac.uk/docs/oncology/other/Good%20Practice%20Guide%20for%20Clinical%20Oncologists.htm

19. Making your chemotherapy service more patient-friendly, 2nd Edition. London. The Royal College of Radiologists, 2008. www.rcr.ac.uk/docs/oncology/pdf/PatientChemo_web.pdf

20. Consent: Patients and Doctors Making Decisions Together. 2008. general Medical Council. London. http://www.gmc-uk.org.uk

21. Department of Health. 2001. Good practice in consent: achieving the NHS Plan commitment to patient-centred consent practice. 2001. London. http://www.dh.gov.uk/en/Publichealth/Scientificdevelopmentgeneticsandbioethics/Consent/Consentgeneralinformation/index.htm

22. Treleaven J, Cullis JO, Maynard R et al for the British Committee for Standards in Haematology. Obtaining consent for chemotherapy. 2005. British Journal of Haematology, 132, 552–559 www.bcshguidelines.com/pdf/consent_15112006.pdf

23. High quality care for all: NHS Next Stage Review final report. 2008. Department of Health http://www.dh.gov.uk/en/publicationsandstatistics/publications/publicationspolicyandguidance/DH_085825

24. Census of Consultant Physicians in the UK. 2006. Royal College of Physicians of London http://www.rcplondon.ac.uk/pubs/epubs.aspx

25. End of Life Care Strategy Promoting high quality care for all adults at the end of life July 2008. Department of Health www.dh.gov.uk/publications

26. Acutely ill patients in hospital. NICE Clinical Guideline 50. 2008. National Institute for Health and Clinical Excellence.

27. Good Medical Practice. 2006. General Medical Council. London http://www.gmc-uk.org/guidance/good_medical_practice/index.asp

28. National Cancer Peer Review Programme. 2004-07. Department of Health. London http://www.qub.ac.uk/research-centres/nicr/FileStore/PDF/Filetoupload,90548,en.pdf

29. Palliative care services: meeting the needs of patients. Report of a Working Party. Royal College of Physicians. London: RCP, 2007.

30. O'Brien MER, Borthwick A, Rigg A et al. Mortality within 30 days of chemotherapy: a clinical governance benchmarking issue for oncology patients. British Journal of Cancer (2006) 95, 1632-1636.

31. Audrey S, Abel J, Blazeby J et al. What oncologists tell patients about survival benefits of palliative chemotherapy and implications for informed consent: qualitative study. British Medical Journal 2008; 337: 492-496

Appendices

Appendix 1 – Glossary

Adjuvant therapy
SACT given following surgery where tumour has been completely resected and there is no evidence of metastatic disease.

Cancer centre
Provides expertise in the management of all cancers including common cancers within their immediate locality and less common cancers by referral from cancer units. They provide specialist diagnostic and therapeutic techniques including radiotherapy.

Cancer unit
Supports clinical teams with sufficient expertise and facilities to manage the more common cancers.

Chemotherapy extravasation
Leakage of a drug out of a vein and into the surrounding tissues.

Course
A course of one type of treatment each course lasting for example between 3 and 6 months.

CVL
Central venous line.

Cycle
Each course of treatment consists of several cycles - for example, one course could consist of four, three-weekly cycles.

FBC
Full blood count.

GCSF
Granulocyte colony-stimulating factor. A growth factor that stimulates the bone marrow to make neutrophils and some other types of white blood cells. It is also known as filgrastim.

GFR
Glomerular filtration rate.

Grade 3/4 – grade of toxicity
A grading system used to record the severity of treatment related side effects (Appendix 5).

HDU
High dependency unit – an area for patients who require more intensive observation, treatment and nursing care than can be provided on a general ward.

High dose palliative SACT
Where SACT is not necessarily curative but remissions can last years.

ICU (ITU)
Intensive care unit (Intensive therapy unit) - an area to which patients are admitted for treatment of actual or impending organ failure.

JCCO
Joint Collegiate Council for Oncology.

Line of therapy
Each new course of treatment. The first course of treatment is referred to as "first line therapy". Subsequent courses, consisting of different combinations of drugs, are referred to as "second line", "third line" or "fourth line" therapy.

LFT
Liver fuction test.

Neo-adjuvant therapy
SACT prior to surgery and/or radiotherapy.

Palliative SACT
SACT given with the aim of symptom control, improvement in the quality of life, tumour growth restraint or increased survival times.

Parenteral
Administered by means other than through the alimentary tract.

RFT
Renal function test.

SACT
Systemic anti-cancer therapy.

WCC
White cell count.

Appendix 2 – SACT regimens

CHOP
Cyclophosphamide
Doxorubicin
Vincristine
Prednisone

R-CHOP
Cyclophosphamide
Doxorubicin
Vincristine
Prednisone
Rituximab

CarboEtop
Carboplatin
Etoposide

GemCarbo
Gemcitabine
Carboplatin

ECX
Epirubicin
Cisplatin
Capecitabine

ECF
Epirubicin
Cisplatin
5- Fluorouracil

CisP 5FU
Cisplatin
5-Fluorouracil

Appendix 3 – Drugs included

SACT - list of drugs - alphabetical order

Aldesleukin (Proleukin)
Alemtuzumab (MabCampath)
Amsacrine (Amsidine)
Anagrelide
Arsenic trioxide (Trisenox)
Bevacizumab (Avastin)
Bexarotene (Targretin)
Bleomycin (Bleomycin)
Bortezomib (Velcade)
Busulfan (Busilvex, Myleran)
Capecitabine (Xeloda)
Carboplatin (Carboplatin, Paraplatin)
Carmustine (BiCNU, Gliadel)
Cetuximab (Erbitux)
Chlorambucil (Leukeran)
Cisplatin (Cisplatin)
Cladribine (Leustat)
Crisantaspase (Erwinase)

Cyclophosphamide (Cyclophosphamide, Endoxana)
Cytarabine (Cytarabine, DepoCyte)
Dacarbazine (Dacarbazine, DTIC-Dome)
Dactinomycin (Cosmegen Lyovac)
Daunorubicin (Daunorubicin, DaunoXome)
Docetaxel (Taxotere)
Doxorubicin Hydrochloride (Doxorubicin Rapid Dissolution, Doxorubicin Solution for Injection, Caelyx, Myocet)
Epirubicin Hydrochloride (Pharmorubicin Rapid Dissolution, Pharmorubicin Solution for Injection)
Estramustine Phosphate (Estracyt)
Etoposide (Etoposide, Etopophos, Vepesid)
Fludarabine Phosphate (Fludara)
Fluorouracil (Fluorouracil, Efudix)
Gemcitabine (Gemzar)
Hydroxycarbamide (Hydroxycarbamide, Hydrea)
Ibritumomab (Zevalin)
Idarubicin Hydrochloride (Zavedos)
Ifosfamide (Mitoxana)
Imatinib (Glivec)
Interferon alpha (IntronA, Roferon-A, Veraferon)
Irinotecan hydrochloride (Campto)
Lenolidomide (Revlimid)
Lomustine (Lomustine)
Melphalan (Alkeran)
Mercaptopurine (Puri-Nethol)
Methotrexate (Methotrexate)
Mitobronitolm (Myelobromol, Durbin)
Mitomycin (Mitomycin C Kyowa)
Mitoxantrone (Mitoxantrone, Novantrone, Onkotrone)
Oxaliplatin (Eloxatin)
Paclitaxel (Paclitaxel, Taxol)
Pemetrexed (Alimta)
Pentostatin (Nipent)
Porfimer sodium (Photofrin)
Procarbazine (Procarbazine)
Raltitrexed (Tomudex)
Rituximab (MabThera)
Tegafur with Uracil (Uftoral)
Temoporfin (Foscan)

Temozolomide (Temodal)
Thalidomide
Thiotepa (Thiotepa)
Tioguanine (Lanvis)
Topotecan (Hycamtin)
Tositumomab (Bexxar)
Trastuzumab (Herceptin)
Treosulfan (Treosulfan)
Tretinoin (Vesanoid)
Vinblastine sulphate (Vinblastine, Velbe)
Vincristine sulphate (Vincristine, Oncovin)
Vindesine sulphate (Eldisine)
Vinorelbine (Navelbine)
Zevalin

Appendix 4 – Tumour response

RECIST (Response Evaluation Criteria In Solid Tumours) Response Definitions

1) Complete response (CR): disappearance of all lesions determined by 2 observations not less than 2 weeks apart;

2) Partial response (PR): ≥30% decrease in the sum of longest diameters of target lesions compared to baseline, with response or stable disease observed in non-target lesions, and no new lesions;

3) Stable disease (SD): neither sufficient shrinkage to qualify for response or sufficient increase to qualify for progressive disease in target lesions, with response or stable disease observed in non-target lesions, and no new lesions;

4) Progressive disease (PD): ≥20% increase in the sum of longest diameters of target lesions compared to smallest sum longest diameter recorded, or unequivocal progression of non-target lesions, or appearance of new lesions.

Appendix 5 – Common Toxicity Criteria

Toxicity	0	1	2	3	4	5
A) GASTROINTESTINAL						
Stomatitis (functional/ symptomatic)	None	Minimal discomfort, intervention not indicated	Symptomatic, medical intervention indicated but not interfering with ADL	Stool incontinence or other symptoms interfering with ADL	Symptoms associated with life-threatening consequences	Death
Nausea	None	Loss of appetite without alteration in eating habits	Oral intake decreased without significant weight loss, dehydration or malnutrition; IV fluids indicated <24hrs	Inadequate oral caloric or fluid intake; IV fluids, tube feedings, or TPN indicated ≥24hrs	Life-threatening consequences	Death
Vomiting	None	1 episode in 24 hours	2-5 episodes in 24 hours; IV fluids indicated <24hrs	≥ 6 episodes in 24 hours; IV fluids, or TPN indicated ≥ 24hrs	Life-threatening consequences	Death
Diarrhoea (patients without colostomy)	None	Increase of <4 stools/ day over baseline	Increase of 4-6 stools/ day over baseline; IV fluids indicated <24hrs	Increase of ≥7 stools/ day; incontinence; IV fluids ≥24hrs; hospitalisation	Life-threatening consequences (e.g. haemodynamic collapse)	Death
Diarrhoea (patients with a colostomy)	None	Mild increase in ostomy output compared with baseline	Moderate increase in ostomy output compared with baseline, not interfering with ADL	Severe increase in ostomy output compared to baseline, interfering with ADL	Life-threatening consequences (e.g. haemodynamic collapse)	Death
B) HAEMATOLOGICAL						
Haemoglobin	Within normal limits	10.0g/dl – normal	8.0 - 9.9g/dl	6.5 - 7.9g/dl	<6.5g/dl	Death
Platelets	Within normal limits	75x109/1 – normal	50 – 74x109/1	25 – 49x109/1	<25x109/1	Death
WBC	Within normal limits	3.0x109/1 – normal	2.0 – 2.9x109/1	1.0 – 1.9x109/1	<1.0x109/1	Death
Neutrophils	Within normal limits	1.5x109/1 – normal	1.0 – 1.4x109/1	0.5 – 0.9x109/1	<0.5x109/1	Death

Toxicity (cont)	0	1	2	3	4	5
C) EFFECT OF BLOOD DISORDERS						
Febrile neutropaenia (ANC<1.0 x109/L, fever ≥38.5°C)	Within normal limits	-	-	Present	Life threatening consequences (e.g. septic shock, hypotension, acidosis, necrosis)	Death
Infection with grade 3 or 4 neutrophils (ANC<1.0 x109/L)	Within normal limits	-	Localised, local intervention indicated	IV antibiotic, antifungal, or antiviral intervention indicated; interventional radiology or operative intervention indicated	Life threatening consequences (e.g. septic shock, hypotension, acidosis, necrosis)	Death
Infection with normal ANC or grade 1 or 2 neutrophils	Within normal limits	-	Localised, local intervention indicated	IV antibiotic, antifungal, or antiviral intervention indicated; interventional radiology or operative intervention indicated	Life threatening consequences (e.g. septic shock, hypotension, acidosis, necrosis)	Death
Haemorrhage/bleeding (other)	Within normal limits	Mild without transfusion	-	Transfusion indicated	Catastrophic bleeding, requiring major non-elective intervention	Death
Thrombosis/embolism (vascular access related)	Within normal limits	-	Deep vein thrombosis or cardiac thrombosis; intervention (e.g. anticoagulation, lysis, filter, invasive procedure) not indicated	Deep vein thrombosis or cardiac thrombosis; intervention (e.g. anticoagulation, lysis, filter, invasive procedure) indicated	Embolic event including pulmonary embolism or life-threatening thrombus	Death
Thrombosis/thrombus/embolism	Within normal limits	-	Deep vein thrombosis or cardiac thrombosis; intervention (e.g. anticoagulation, lysis, filter, invasive procedure) not indicated	Deep vein thrombosis or cardiac thrombosis; intervention (e.g. anticoagulation, lysis, filter, invasive procedure) indicated	Embolic event including pulmonary embolism or life-threatening thrombus	Death

Toxicity (cont)	0	1	2	3	4	5
D) METABOLIC DISORDERS						
Sodium, serum-high (hypernatraemia)	Within normal limits	->ULN – 150 mmol/L	>150 – 155 mmol/L	>155 – 160 mmol/L	>160 mmol/L	Death
Sodium, serum-low (hyponatraemia)	Within normal limits	<LLN – 130 mmol/L	-	<130 – 120 mmol/L	<120 mmol/L	Death
Potassium, serum-high (hyperkalaemia)	Within normal limits	>ULN – 5.5 mmol/L	>5.5 – 6.0 mmol/L	>6.0 – 7.0 mmol/L	>7.0 mmol/L	Death
Potassium, serum-low (hypokalaemia)	Within normal limits	<LLN – 3.0 mmol/L	-	<3.0 – 2.5 mmol/L	<2.5 mmol/L	
Magnesium, serum-high (hypermagnesaemia)	Within normal limits	>ULN – 3.0 mg/dL >ULN – 1.23 mmol/L	-	>3.0 – 8.0 mg/dL >1.23 – 3.30 mmol/L	>8.0 mg/dL >3.30 mmol/L	Death
Magnesium, serum-low (hypomagnesaemia)	Within normal limits	<LLN – 1.2 mg/dL <LLN – 0.5 mmol/L	<1.2 – 0.9 mg/dL <0.5 – 0.4 mmol/L	<0.9 – 0.7 mg/dL <0.4 – 0.3 mmol/L	<0.7 mg/dL <0.3 mmol/L	Death
Calcium, serum-high (hypercalcaemia)	Within normal limits	>ULN – 11.5 mg/dL >ULN – 2.9 mmol/L Ionised calcium: >ULN – 1.5 mmol/L	>11.5 – 12.5 mg/dL >2.9 – 3.1 mmol/L Ionised calcium: >1.5 – 1.6 mmol/L	>12.5 – 13.5 mg/dL >3.1 – 3.4 mmol/L Ionised calcium: >1.6 – 1.8 mmol/L	>13.5 mg/dL >3.4 mmol/L Ionised calcium: >1.8 mmol/L	Death
Calcium, serum-low (hypocalcaemia)	Within normal limits	<LLN – 8.0 mg/dL <LLN – 2.0 mmol/L Ionised calcium: <LLN – 1.0 mmol/L	<8.0 – 7.0 mg/dL <2.0 – 1.75 mmol/L Ionised calcium: <1.0 – 0.9 mmol/L	<7.0 – 6.0 mg/dL <1.75 – 1.5 mmol/L Ionised calcium: <0.9 - 0.8 mmol/L	<6.0 mg/dL <1.5 mmol/L Ionised calcium: <0.8 mmol/L	Death
Creatinine	Within normal limits	>ULN – 1.5 x ULN	>1.5 – 3.0 x ULN	>3.0 – 6.0 x ULN	>6.0 x ULN	Death
Bilirubin (hyperbilirubinaemia)	Within normal limits	>ULN – 1.5 x ULN	>1.5 – 3.0 x ULN	>3.0 – 10.0 x ULN	>10.0 x ULN	Death
ALT/AST	Within normal limits	>ULN – 2.5 x ULN	>2.5 – 5.0 x ULN	>5.0 – 20.0 x ULN	>20.0 x ULN	Death

Toxicity (cont)	0	1	2	3	4	5
E) NEUROLOGICAL						
Sensory neuropathy	Normal	Asymptomatic; loss of deep tendon reflexes or paresthesia (including tingling) but not interfering with function	Sensory alteration or paresthesia (including tingling), interfering with function, but not interfering with ADL	Sensory alteration or paresthesia interfering with ADL	Disabling	Death
Motor neuropathy	Normal	Asymptomatic; weakness on exam/ testing only	Symptomatic weakness interfering with function, but not interfering with ADL	Weakness interfering with ADL; bracing or assistance to walk indicated	Life-threatening; disabling (e.g. paralysis)	Death
F) CARDIAC						
Cardiac ischaemia/ infarction	None	Asymptomatic arterial narrowing without ischaemia	Asymptomatic and testing suggesting ischaemia; stable angina	Symptomatic and testing consistent with ischaemia; unstable angina; intervention indicated	Acute myocardial infarction	Death
Cardiac arrhythmia	None	Mild	Moderate	Severe	Life-threatening; disabling	Death
G) OTHER						
Allergic reaction/hyper-sensitivity (including drug fever)	Normal	Transient flushing or rash; drug fever <38°C (<100.4°F)	Rash; flushing urticaria; dyspnea; drug fever ≥38°C (≥100.4°F)	Symptomatic bronchospasm, with or without urticaria; parenteral medication(s) indicated; allergy-related edema/angioedema; hypotension	Anaphylaxis	Death
Pain	None	Mild pain not interfering with function	Moderate pain: pain or analgesics interfering with function, but not interfering with ADL	Severe pain: pain or analgesics severely interfering with ADL	Disabling	-
Rash: hand-foot skin reaction	None	Minimal skin changes or dermatitis (e.g. erythema) without pain	Skin changes (e.g. peeling, blisters, bleeding, oedema) or pain, not interfering with function	Ulcerative dermatitis or skin changes with pain, interfering with function	-	-
Tumour lysis syndrome	None	-	-	Present	-	Death

Appendix 6 – Hours of work

Day	08:00 to 17:59
Evening	18:00 to 23:59
Night	00:00 to 07:59

Office hours	08:00 to 17:59 Monday to Friday
Out of hours	18:00 to 07:59 Monday to Friday and all day Saturday and Sunday

Appendix 7 – Inclusion ICD-10 codes

All patients who died with the following ICD-10 codes recorded anywhere in their diagnosis were included

C00 - 97	Malignant neoplasms (including C81 Hodgkin's disease, C92 myeloid leukaemia)
D37 - 48	Neoplasm of uncertain or unknown behaviour
C90	Multiple myeloma and malignant plasma cell neoplasms
C91.1	Chronic lymphocytic leukaemia
C92.1	Chronic myeloid leukaemia
C93.1	Chronic monocytic leukaemia
C94.1	Chronic erythraemia
C95.1	Chronic leukaemia of unspecified cell type
D00-D02, D04-07, D09	Carcinomas
D46	Myelodysplastic syndromes
D47	Other neoplasms of uncertain or unknown behaviour of lymphoid, haematopoietic and related tissue (includes chronic myeloproliferative disease).

Appendix 8 – Corporate structure

The National Confidential Enquiry into Patient Outcome and Death (NCEPOD) is an independent body to which a corporate commitment has been made by the Medical and Surgical Colleges, Associations and Faculties related to its area of activity. Each of these bodies nominates members on to NCEPOD's Steering Group.

Steering Group as at 12th November 2008

Dr D Whitaker	Association of Anaesthetists of Great Britain & Ireland
Mr T Bates	Association of Surgeons of Great Britain & Ireland
Mr J Wardrope	College of Emergency Medicine
Dr S Bridgman	Faculty of Public Health Medicine
Dr P Cartwright	Royal College of Anaesthetists
Dr P Nightingale	Royal College of Anaesthetists
Dr B Ellis	Royal College of General Practitioners
Ms M McElligott	Royal College of Nursing
Professor D Luesley	Royal College of Obstetricians and Gynaecologists
Mrs M Wishart	Royal College of Ophthalmologists
Dr I Doughty	Royal College of Paediatrics and Child Health
Dr R Dowdle	Royal College of Physicians
Professor T Hendra	Royal College of Physicians
Dr M Armitage	Royal College of Physicians
Dr M Clements	Royal College of Physicians
Dr S McPherson	Royal College of Radiologists
Mr B Rees	Royal College of Surgeons of England
Mr M Parker	Royal College of Surgeons of England
Mr D Mitchell	Faculty of Dental Surgery, Royal College of Surgeons of England
Dr S Lishman	Royal College of Pathologists
Ms S Panizzo	Patient Representative
Mrs M Wang	Patient Representative

Observers

Mrs C Miles	Institute of Healthcare Management
Dr R Palmer	Coroners' Society of England and Wales
Mrs H Burton	Scottish Audit of Surgical Mortality
Dr K Cleary	National Patient Safety Agency
Ms R Brown	National Patient Safety Agency
Professor P Littlejohns	National Institute for Health and Clinical Excellence

NCEPOD is a company, limited by guarantee and a registered charity, managed by Trustees.

Trustees

Chairman	Professor T Treasure
Treasurer	Professor G T Layer
	Professor M Britton
	Professor J H Shepherd
	Mr M A M S Leigh
	Dr D Justins
Company Secretary	Dr M Mason

Clinical Co-ordinators

The Steering Group appoint a Lead Clinical Co-ordinator for a defined tenure. In addition there are eight Clinical Co-ordinators who work on each study. All Co-ordinators are engaged in active academic/clinical practice (in the NHS) during their term of office.

Lead Clinical Co-ordinator	Mr I C Martin (Surgery)
Clinical Co-ordinators	Dr D G Mason (Anaesthesia)
	Dr K Wilkinson (Anaesthesia)
	Dr A Goodwin (Anaesthesia)
	Dr J A D Stewart (Medicine)
	Professor S B Lucas (Pathology)
	Dr G Findlay (Intensive Care)
	Dr D Mort (Oncology)
	Mr M Lansdown (Surgery)

Appendix 9 – Participation

Organisation	SACT data	Death data	QA sent	QA returned	QB sent	QB returned	Org Q returned
Aintree Hospitals NHS Trust	Yes	Yes	4	4	4	4	Yes
Airedale NHS Trust	Yes	Yes	9	9	9	8	Yes
Ashford & St Peter's Hospital NHS Trust	Yes	Yes	2	2	2	2	Yes
Aspen Healthcare	Yes	Yes	0	0	0	0	Yes
Barnet and Chase Farm Hospitals NHS Trust	No	No	0	0	0	0	No
Barts and The London NHS Trust	Yes	Yes	25	6	25	9	Yes
Basildon & Thurrock University Hospitals NHS Foundation Trust	Yes	Yes	4	4	4	4	Yes
Bedford Hospital NHS Trust	Yes	Yes	1	1	1	0	Yes
Blackpool, Fylde and Wyre Hospitals NHS Trust	Yes	Yes	5	4	5	4	Yes
BMI Healthcare	Yes	Yes	5	1	5	1	Yes
Bolton Hospitals NHS Trust	Yes	Yes	5	2	5	3	Yes
Bradford Teaching Hospitals NHS Foundation Trust	Yes	Yes	3	3	3	3	Yes
Brighton and Sussex University Hospitals NHS Trust	Yes	Yes	5	1	5	3	Yes
Bromley Hospitals NHS Trust	Yes	Yes	0	0	0	0	Yes
Buckinghamshire Hospitals NHS Trust	Yes	Yes	9	7	9	6	Yes
BUPA	No	Yes	2	0	2	0	Yes
Burton Hospitals NHS Trust	Yes	Yes	4	4	4	4	Yes
Calderdale & Huddersfield NHS Trust	Yes	Yes	0	0	0	0	No
Cambridge University Hospitals NHS Foundation Trust	Yes	Yes	11	5	11	5	Yes
Capio Healthcare UK	Yes	Yes	2	1	2	1	Yes
Cardiff and Vale NHS Trust	Yes	Yes	0	0	0	0	Yes
Carmarthenshire NHS Trust	Yes	Yes	1	1	1	0	Yes
Central Manchester & Manchester Children's NHS Trust	Yes	Yes	2	2	2	2	Yes
Ceredigion & Mid Wales NHS Trust	Yes	Yes	3	3	3	3	Yes
Chelsea & Westminster Healthcare NHS Trust	Yes	Yes	3	1	3	1	Yes
Chesterfield Royal Hospital NHS Foundation Trust	Yes	Yes	1	1	1	1	Yes
Christie Hospital NHS Trust	Yes	Yes	53	46	53	45	Yes

Participation (Cont)

Organisation	SACT data	Death data	QA sent	QA returned	QB sent	QB returned	Org Q returned
City Hospitals Sunderland NHS Foundation Trust	Yes	Yes	8	8	8	8	Yes
Classic Hospitals	Yes	Yes	0	0	0	0	Yes
Clatterbridge Centre for Oncology NHS Trust	Yes	Yes	34	29	34	29	Yes
Conwy & Denbighshire NHS Trust	Yes	Yes	10	10	10	9	Yes
Countess of Chester Hospital NHS Foundation Trust	Yes	Yes	1	1	1	1	Yes
County Durham and Darlington Acute Hospitals NHS Trust	Yes	Yes	1	1	1	1	Yes
Covenant Healthcare Limted	Yes	Yes	0	0	0	0	Yes
Dartford & Gravesham NHS Trust	Yes	No	0	0	0	0	Yes
Derby Hospitals NHS Foundation Trust	Yes	Yes	18	7	18	8	Yes
Doncaster and Bassetlaw Hospitals NHS Foundation Trust	Yes	Yes	0	0	0	0	Yes
Dorset County Hospital NHS Foundation Trust	Yes	Yes	9	9	9	7	Yes
Dudley Group of Hospitals NHS Trust	Yes	Yes	6	3	6	2	Yes
Ealing Hospital NHS Trust	Yes	Yes	0	0	0	0	Yes
East Cheshire NHS Trust	Yes	Yes	3	0	3	1	Yes
East Lancashire Hospitals NHS Trust	Yes	No	0	0	0	0	Yes
East Sussex Hospitals NHS Trust	Yes	Yes	7	6	7	5	Yes
Epsom and St Helier University Hospitals NHS Trust	Yes	Yes	2	1	2	0	Yes
Essex Rivers Healthcare NHS Trust	Yes	Yes	12	12	12	12	Yes
Frimley Park Hospitals NHS Trust	Yes	No	0	0	0	0	Yes
Gateshead Health NHS Trust	Yes	Yes	2	1	2	0	Yes
George Eliot Hospital NHS Trust	Yes	Yes	7	3	7	4	Yes
Gloucestershire Hospitals NHS Foundation Trust	Yes	Yes	0	0	34	1	Yes
Guy's & St Thomas' NHS Foundation Trust	Yes	Yes	5	0	5	2	Yes
Gwent Healthcare NHS Trust	Yes	Yes	4	3	4	3	Yes
Hampshire Primary Care Trust	Yes	Yes	0	0	0	0	No
Harrogate and District NHS Foundation Trust	Yes	Yes	4	3	4	4	Yes
HCA International	Yes	Yes	1	0	1	0	Yes
Health & Social Services, States of Guernsey	Yes	Yes	1	1	1	1	Yes
Heart of England NHS Foundation Trust	Yes	Yes	6	3	6	3	Yes

Participation (Cont)

Organisation	SACT data	Death data	QA sent	QA returned	QB sent	QB returned	Org Q returned
Heatherwood and Wexham Park Hospitals NHS Trust	Yes	Yes	7	6	7	6	Yes
Hereford Hospitals NHS Trust	Yes	Yes	0	0	0	0	Yes
Hillingdon Hospital NHS Trust	Yes	Yes	0	0	0	0	Yes
Hinchingbrooke Health Care NHS Trust	Yes	Yes	3	3	3	3	Yes
Homerton University Hospital NHS Foundation Trust	Yes	Yes	0	0	0	0	Yes
Hull and East Yorkshire Hospitals NHS Trust	Yes	Yes	14	6	14	7	Yes
Imperial College Healthcare NHS Trust	Yes	Yes	38	16	38	16	Yes
Ipswich Hospital NHS Trust	No	Yes	0	0	0	0	Yes
Isle of Wight Healthcare NHS Trust	Yes	Yes	5	3	5	4	Yes
James Paget Healthcare NHS Trust	Yes	Yes	6	5	6	6	Yes
Kettering General Hospital NHS Trust	Yes	Yes	0	0	0	0	Yes
King's College Hospital NHS Trust	Yes	Yes	6	4	6	5	Yes
Kingston Hospital NHS Trust	Yes	Yes	2	2	2	2	Yes
Lancashire Teaching Hospitals NHS Foundation Trust	Yes	Yes	18	13	18	12	Yes
Leeds Teaching Hospitals NHS Trust	Yes	Yes	15	12	15	12	Yes
Leicestershire County and Rutland Primary Care Trust	Yes	Yes	0	0	0	0	Yes
Lewisham Hospital NHS Trust	Yes	Yes	1	0	1	0	Yes
Luton and Dunstable Hospital NHS Trust	Yes	Yes	5	5	5	5	Yes
Maidstone and Tunbridge Wells NHS Trust	Yes	Yes	5	4	5	4	Yes
Mayday Health Care NHS Trust	Yes	Yes	0	0	0	0	Yes
Medway NHS Trust	Yes	Yes	1	0	1	1	Yes
Mid Cheshire Hospitals NHS Trust	Yes	Yes	0	0	0	0	Yes
Mid Essex Primary Care Trust	Yes	Yes	0	0	0	0	Yes
Mid Staffordshire General Hospitals NHS Trust	Yes	Yes	0	0	0	0	Yes
Mid Yorkshire Hospitals NHS Trust	Yes	Yes	3	1	3	0	Yes
Mid-Essex Hospital Services NHS Trust	Yes	Yes	7	4	7	3	Yes
Milton Keynes Hospital NHS Foundation Trust	Yes	Yes	3	3	3	3	Yes
Newcastle upon Tyne Hospitals NHS Trust	Yes	Yes	9	9	9	9	Yes
Newham Healthcare NHS Trust	Yes	Yes	1	0	1	0	Yes
Norfolk & Norwich University Hospital NHS Trust	Yes	Yes	14	13	14	11	Yes

Participation (Cont)

Organisation	SACT data	Death data	QA sent	QA returned	QB sent	QB returned	Org Q returned
Norfolk Primary Care Trust	Yes	Yes	0	0	0	0	Yes
North Bristol NHS Trust	Yes	Yes	3	2	3	2	Yes
North Cheshire Hospitals NHS Trust	Yes	Yes	0	0	0	0	Yes
North Cumbria Acute Hospitals NHS Trust	Yes	Yes	0	0	0	0	Yes
North East Wales NHS Trust	Yes	Yes	3	1	3	1	Yes
North Glamorgan NHS Trust	Yes	No	0	0	0	0	Yes
North Middlesex University Hospital NHS Trust	Yes	Yes	3	2	3	2	Yes
North Tees and Hartlepool NHS Trust	Yes	Yes	5	4	5	4	Yes
North West London Hospitals NHS Trust	Yes	Yes	3	3	3	3	Yes
North West Wales NHS Trust	Yes	No	0	0	0	0	Yes
North Yorkshire and York Primary Care Trust	Yes	Yes	0	0	0	0	
Northampton General Hospital NHS Trust	Yes	Yes	6	6	6	6	Yes
Northern Devon Healthcare NHS Trust	Yes	Yes	0	0	0	0	Yes
Northern Lincolnshire & Goole Hospitals Trust	Yes	Yes	3	1	3	0	Yes
Northumbria Healthcare NHS Trust	Yes	Yes	0	0	0	0	Yes
Nottingham University Hospitals NHS Trust	Yes	Yes	7	1	7	1	Yes
Nuffield	Yes	Yes	2	1	2	1	Yes
Oxford Radcliffe Hospital NHS Trust	Yes	Yes	0	0	0	0	No
Pembrokeshire & Derwen NHS Trust	Yes	Yes	2	2	2	1	Yes
Pennine Acute Hospitals NHS Trust	Yes	Yes	6	1	6	1	Yes
Peterborough & Stamford Hospitals NHS Foundation Trust	Yes	Yes	3	3	3	2	Yes
Plymouth Hospitals NHS Trust	Yes	Yes	14	7	14	7	Yes
Plymouth Primary Care Trust	Yes	Yes	0	0	0	0	Yes
Poole Hospital NHS Trust	Yes	Yes	10	2	10	0	Yes
Portsmouth Hospitals NHS Trust	Yes	Yes	20	20	20	15	Yes
Princess Alexandra Hospital NHS Trust	Yes	Yes	2	2	2	2	Yes
Queen Elizabeth Hospital NHS Trust	Yes	Yes	4	2	4	2	Yes
Queen Mary's Sidcup NHS Trust	Yes	Yes	2	1	2	1	Yes
Redcar and Cleveland Primary Care Trust	No	Yes	0	0	0	0	No
Royal Berkshire NHS Foundation Trust	Yes	Yes	18	5	18	11	Yes
Royal Bournemouth and Christchurch Hospitals NHS Trust	Yes	Yes	0	0	0	0	Yes
Royal Cornwall Hospitals NHS Trust	Yes	Yes	12	12	12	12	Yes

Participation (Cont)

Organisation	SACT data	Death data	QA sent	QA returned	QB sent	QB returned	Org Q returned
Royal Devon and Exeter NHS Foundation Trust	Yes	Yes	5	5	5	5	Yes
Royal Liverpool and Broadgreen University Hospitals NHS Trust	Yes	Yes	1	1	1	1	Yes
Royal Marsden NHS Foundation Trust	Yes	Yes	25	21	25	19	Yes
Royal Surrey County Hospital NHS Trust	Yes	Yes	10	10	10	9	Yes
Royal United Hospital Bath NHS Trust	Yes	Yes	9	4	9	4	Yes
Royal West Sussex NHS Trust	Yes	Yes	5	1	5	1	Yes
Royal Wolverhampton Hospitals NHS Trust	Yes	Yes	14	6	14	8	Yes
Salford Royal Hospitals NHS Trust	Yes	Yes	1	1	1	0	Yes
Salisbury Foundation NHS Trust	Yes	Yes	2	2	2	2	Yes
Sandwell and West Birmingham Hospitals NHS Trust	Yes	Yes	8	4	8	4	Yes
Scarborough and North East Yorkshire Health Care NHS Trust	Yes	Yes	4	2	4	3	Yes
Sheffield Teaching Hospitals NHS Foundation Trust	Yes	Yes	33	33	33	32	Yes
Sherwood Forest Hospitals NHS Trust	Yes	Yes	0	0	0	0	Yes
Shrewsbury and Telford Hospitals NHS Trust	Yes	Yes	9	8	9	7	Yes
South Devon Healthcare NHS Trust	Yes	Yes	9	8	9	6	Yes
South Tees Hospitals NHS Trust	Yes	Yes	21	10	21	12	Yes
South Tyneside Healthcare Trust	Yes	Yes	0	0	16	0	Yes
South Warwickshire General Hospitals NHS Trust	Yes	Yes	0	0	0	0	Yes
Southampton University Hospitals NHS Trust	Yes	Yes	16	14	16	14	Yes
Southend Hospital NHS Trust	Yes	Yes	10	3	10	5	Yes
Southern Health & Social Care Trust	Yes	Yes	0	0	0	0	Yes
Southport and Ormskirk Hospitals NHS Trust	Yes	Yes	0	0	0	0	Yes
Spire Healthcare	Yes	Yes	0	0	0	0	Yes
St George's Healthcare NHS Trust	Yes	Yes	11	9	11	9	Yes
St Helens and Knowsley Hospitals NHS Trust	Yes	Yes	1	1	1	1	Yes
Stockport NHS Foundation Trust	Yes	Yes	1	0	1	0	Yes
Surrey & Sussex Healthcare NHS Trust	Yes	Yes	2	2	2	2	Yes
Swansea NHS Trust	Yes	Yes	0	0	0	0	Yes
Swindon & Marlborough NHS Trust	Yes	Yes	4	4	4	4	Yes

Participation (Cont)

Organisation	SACT data	Death data	QA sent	QA returned	QB sent	QB returned	Org Q returned
Tameside and Glossop Acute Services NHS Trust	Yes	Yes	0	0	0	0	Yes
Taunton & Somerset NHS Trust	Yes	Yes	11	11	11	11	Yes
The Queen Elizabeth Hospital King's Lynn NHS Trust	Yes	Yes	8	8	8	8	Yes
The Rotherham NHS Foundation Trust	Yes	Yes	1	1	1	1	Yes
Trafford Healthcare NHS Trust	Yes	Yes	1	1	1	1	
Trafford Primary Care Trust	Yes	Yes	0	0	0	0	Yes
United Bristol Healthcare NHS Trust	Yes	Yes	17	14	17	14	Yes
United Hospitals Health & Social Services Trust	Yes	Yes	0	0	0	0	No
University Hospital of South Manchester NHS Foundation Trust	Yes	Yes	10	0	10	0	Yes
University College London Hospitals NHS Foundation Trust	Yes	Yes	9	3	9	4	Yes
University Hospital Birmingham NHS Foundation Trust	Yes	Yes	4	3	4	4	Yes
University Hospitals Coventry and Warwickshire NHS Trust	Yes	Yes	17	16	17	16	Yes
University Hospitals of Leicester NHS Trust	Yes	Yes	30	12	30	12	Yes
University Hospitals of Morecambe Bay NHS Trust	Yes	Yes	7	6	7	6	No
Velindre NHS Trust	Yes	Yes	18	12	18	12	Yes
Walsall Hospitals NHS Trust	Yes	Yes	3	2	3	1	Yes
West Hertfordshire Hospitals NHS Trust	Yes	No	0	0	0	0	No
West Middlesex University Hospital NHS Trust	Yes	Yes	1	0	1	0	Yes
West Suffolk Hospitals NHS Trust	Yes	Yes	4	4	4	4	Yes
West Sussex Primary Care Trust	Yes	Yes	0	0	0	0	No
Western Health & Social Care Trust	Yes	No	0	0	0	0	Yes
Weston Area Health Trust	Yes	Yes	1	1	1	1	Yes
Whittington Hospital NHS Trust	Yes	Yes	4	4	4	4	Yes
Winchester & Eastleigh Healthcare NHS Trust	Yes	Yes	1	0	1	1	Yes
Wirral Hospital NHS Trust	Yes	Yes	3	3	3	3	Yes
Worcestershire Acute Hospitals	Yes	Yes	12	9	12	10	Yes
Worthing and Southlands Hospitals NHS Trust	Yes	Yes	3	2	3	3	Yes

Participation (Cont)

Organisation	SACT data	Death data	QA sent	QA returned	QB sent	QB returned	Org Q returned
Wrightington, Wigan & Leigh NHS Trust	Yes	Yes	1	1	1	1	Yes
Yeovil District Hospital NHS FoundationTrust	Yes	Yes	0	0	0	0	Yes
York Hospitals NHS Trust	Yes	Yes	2	2	2	2	Yes

Trusts listed have provided us with data or a report of no data during the study period. A 'Yes' may mean that a notification of no treatment data or no deaths had occurred during the study period.

Please note that Trusts may have more than one site.

Trusts not listed did not provide data; this may have been due to no relevant data during the study.

Where treatment data and/or death data have been returned but no questionnaires have been sent this is because there were no matches of deaths within 30 days of treatment.